The American West

THE AMERICAN WEST

A Narrative Bibliography and a Study in Regionalism

Charles F. Wilkinson

UNIVERSITY PRESS OF COLORADO

The University Press of Colorado is a cooperative publishing enterprise
supported, in part, by Adams State College, Colorado State University, Fort
Lewis College, Mesa State College, Metropolitan State College, University of
Colorado, University of Northern Colorado, University of Southern Colorado, and Western State College.

The paper used in this publication meets the minimum requirements of the
American National Standard for Information Sciences—Permanence of Paper
for Printed Library Materials, ANSI Z39.48–1984.

Library of Congress Cataloging-in-Publication Data

Wilkinson, Charles F., 1941-
The American West: A Narrative Bibliography and a Study in
Regionalism
Bibliography: p.
1. West (U.S.)—Bibliography.
I. Title.
Z1251.W5W52 1989 [F591] 016.978—dc20 89-9044
ISBN 0-87081-204-1. —— ISBN 0-87081-181-9 (pbk.)

Manufactured in the United States of America

I dedicate this book to Wallace Stegner, who has depicted the native home of hope in its truest hues.

CONTENTS

Preface   xi

CHAPTER 1   Defining the West   1

CHAPTER 2   The Events   13
   The Turning Points   15
      The California Gold Rush   15
      The Opening of the Public Domain   17
      The Creation of Yellowstone National Park   18
      Indian Allotment   19
      The Construction of Hoover Dam   20
      The Post–World War II Boom   21
   The Epic Conflicts   22
      Conquest by Manifest Destiny 22
      The Mussel Slough Tragedy   24
      The Johnson County War   25
      Water For Los Angeles   26
      Hetch Hetchy   27
      Alaska Land   28

CHAPTER 3   The People   33
   The Leaders   33
      Lewis and Clark and The Mountain Men   33
      The Big Four   34
      John Wesley Powell   35
      John Muir   35
      Gifford Pinchot   36
      John Collier   37
      Political Figures of the 1960s, 1970s, and 1980s   38
      Wallace Stegner   39
   The Subcultures   41
      American Indians   41

Hispanics   42
Mormons   43
Asian-Americans   44
Farmers, Ranchers, and Cowboys   45
The Institutions   46
The Forest Service   46
The Navajo Nation   47
The Weyerhaeuser Company   48
The Sierra Club   49

CHAPTER 4   The Terrain   53
The Natural Systems   53
The Major Watersheds   53
The Great Plains   55
The Great Basin   56
The Greater Yellowstone Ecosystem   57
The Pacific Coastline   58
Alaska   59
The Commodity Resources   61
Minerals   61
Water   62
Range   63
Timber   64
The Animals and Plants   65
The Grizzly Bear, the Wolf, the Bald Eagle, and the Pa-
cific Salmon   65
Game and Nongame Species   67
Old-Growth Timber Stands   68
Wetlands   69
The Texture of the Ground   70

CHAPTER 5   The Ideas   75
Open Access to Public Natural Resources   75
Resource Planning and Management   77
Land and Species Preservation   78

Market-Based Economics   79
Ethnic Pluralism   80
Cooperation   82
Geologic Time   84

**CHAPTER 6   Postscript: A Word on the Future   89
           of the West**

Bibliography   91

General Reference Works   143

PREFACE

This book probably began in a law firm conference room in Phoenix on a June afternoon in 1966. Paul Roca, a senior partner in Lewis & Roca, gave a talk to all of the firm's lawyers, but especially to the new ones, such as myself, from out of state. Paul, who would become a mentor-friend-father for me, did not talk about the law that day—but, then again, he did. He told us that we needed to know Arizona in order to become fine lawyers in Arizona: law cannot be practiced in a vacuum because it exists in the context of people, history, and places. He then proceeded to give a rich and elaborate lecture on the history, geography, economy, and cultures of the state.

Paul proved his point by example. A Hispanic, he traveled to every part of the Mexican state of Sonora, which shares its northern border with Arizona. He photographed more than one hundred of Sonora's Spanish missions; many of them had been lost to public memory but he personally rediscovered them through the tedious examination of old journals and long jeep trips into the far Sonoran backcountry. Paul then described his travels in the engaging book, *Paths of the Padres Through Sonora* [349]. He had just completed a similar project, *Spanish Jesuit Churches in Mexico's Tarahumara* [350], on Chihuahua, the neighboring state to the east, at the time of his death in 1979. In spite of the massive amounts of time needed to fulfill his avocation as a historian and a latter-day explorer, Paul was a magnificent lawyer, as respected as any attorney in Arizona.

Paul's message in that conference room took hold of me. Having grown up in the East, I knew little about the history or literature of the West—little about the West, period—but I plunged in. The Spanish and Mexican explorers. Lewis and

Clark. The Mormon Trail. The mountain men—oh, the mountain men! When I joined a firm in San Francisco, I immersed myself in the deep and diverse writing of California. Father Junipero Serra. *Two Years Before the Mast*. Dame Shirley. John Muir. Hiram Johnson. Steinbeck. Then I joined the legal staff of the Native American Rights Fund in Boulder and tried to learn about Indians and the Rockies. When I entered academia at the Oregon Law School in 1975, my teaching and research in water, Indian, and federal public land law led me into a beginning exploration of forestry, hydrology, geology, economics, and wildlife biology. If you want to understand the Law of the American West, understand the American West.

All the while I was fortunate to be able to travel throughout the West, visiting clients on Indian reservations and giving public lectures on my fields of specialty. By the time I returned to Boulder in 1987, to the University of Colorado Law School, my ultimate interest had become the places of the West, the philosophy and reality of place, and how law and public policy might further a sense of place. Perhaps I have become so keenly attuned to place because I lack a place. Perhaps I keen to place because the West has become my place.

This book is about the books of the West as I know them. I am no expert, just an eager learner, on many of the subjects I discuss here. My effort has been to identify only readily available works, not the myriad government documents, diaries, doctoral theses, and out-of-print books that afford invaluable depth on individual topics. Nor have I provided complete coverage. The books discussed here are only those that I have read or made myself familar with as resource works through my research. Specialists seeking comprehensive coverage should consult *The Reader's Encyclopedia of the American West* [481] or scholarly bibliographies on topics such as history [482] [483], literature [458] [480], American Indians [333] [334], the frontier [484] [486] [488], the American–Canadian West [485], and the United States–Mexico borderlands [487]. But I have omitted none of my personal favorites, the many books that have enriched my life and allowed me one of life's high luxuries: blending my profession with an adopted place that I have come to love.

This book is about the West as well as its literature. Although many of the works I discuss are important for their literary, historical, scientific, or cultural merits, they also perform the valuable function of helping us understand the special qualities of the region. Thus, I hope that my conceptual approach to this body of literature and the West itself will serve to organize relevant ideas and provide a useful way of thinking about the region and its future.

Let me offer a few words on the format. Each reference in the text is followed by a number. The reader may then find the complete citation to that particular work by looking up the number in the Bibliography at the end of the book. The Bibliography is organized alphabetically and by reference number, and it indicates the page(s) in the text where a specific work is referenced. In addition, I have included a section, General Reference Works, that lists several traditional scholarly bibliographies, historiographies, and encyclopedias.

A great many people—more than I could expressly acknowledge here—have assisted me in this venture. I appreciate the many and varied comments of Tom Watkins, Patty Limerick, John Leshy, Jim Mooney, Larry MacDonnell, Ralph Johnson, Doug Watson, Robert McPhee, and Don Snow. My thanks to my research assistants, Chris Minturn, Sharon Raymond, Karen Lewotsky, Meg Kieran, and Allen Field. Joan Connors and Will Barnes were extraordinary sources of ideas, inspiration, and perspective. Thanks also to the students in my 1987 Advanced Natural Resources Seminar at the Oregon Law School, who discussed their views of the manuscript with me. I also extend my gratitude to the *Michigan Law Review*, which published an earlier version of this piece [464]. Thanks finally to Denis Doyle, Philip Hocker, Lynn Douglas, and Bob Miles, as well as the

Colorado Historical Society, the Wyoming State Archives Museums and Historical Department, and the Native American Rights Fund for the use of their excellent photographs.

CFW
Boulder, Colorado
May, 1989

The American West

Exxon oil and gas drill rig near Jackson Hole, Wyoming with the Teton
Range in the background. 1987, by Philip M. Hocker. Courtesy, Mineral
Policy Center.

DEFINING THE WEST

The American West and its distinctive regional institutions are shaped by the combination of several characteristics of climate, terrain, and political geography. Wallace Stegner, whom I count as the wisest observer of this region, said that the two most influential factors of society in the West are its aridity and its high concentration of federal public lands.[1] Western water, or the lack of it, has determined agricultural, ranch, and mineral development; built financial empires; propelled and limited municipal growth patterns; and inspired recreationists, poets, and citizens of all stripes who are drawn to the rivers, streams, creeks, and rivulets coursing down the steep pitches of western canyons. The public lands matter because of their abundance (they constitute about 50 percent of all land in the eleven western states and nearly 90 percent of Alaska land), their economic value, their intrinsic tendency to create a pattern of dispersed population, and their extraordinary stores of wildlife and beauty.

Other key factors help mold the West's identity. The terrain is variously chopped up by rugged mountains and spread out by high plains and desert country. Further, the region holds most of the nation's Indian lands. The Native American

1

acreage is greater than many Americans realize—almost 6 percent of the eleven western states and, after ongoing transfers of public land to Alaska Natives are completed, 12 percent of Alaska. In addition to the effects of their land holdings and cultural traditions, the tribes also have influenced the region during the past quarter-century by their successes in Congress and the courts, which have solidified Indian resource rights and political power. The rejuvenation of the reservations has sharpened the age-old, uneasy blend of morality, guilt, and melting-pot pragmatism that makes Indianness, and its future, a palpable presence in the West. Similar cultural issues are raised in regard to Hispanic and Mormon settlements, although large land holdings are not involved.

The aridity, the federal public lands, the Indian lands, the mountains, the deserts, and the plains combine to create another influence on western society: open space. Population is moving west but, in a sense, the region is not filling up. The people are settling in the cities, not in the hinterlands—the American West has a higher percentage of its population, approximately 83 percent, residing in metropolitan areas than does any other region. To be sure, the empty quarter is feeling the press of growth, but the awesome space persists. Its tomorrows will be a focal point of the West's law and policy.

There is general agreement that the 100th meridian—running north and south through North Dakota, South Dakota, Nebraska, Kansas, Oklahoma, and Texas—has special significance in defining the geographical reach of the West. The 100th meridian is the dry line, for it roughly represents a key line of rainfall, east of which almost all areas receive more than 20 inches of precipitation annually, west of which almost all of the country receives less than 20 inches. As a rule of thumb, farm crops require 20 inches of precipitation. Agriculture is therefore a far greater challenge, and usually depends on extensive irrigation, in the arid lands to the west of the dry line.

Leading western writers often have articulated the eastern edge of the region in terms of a single person traveling west in

2

the vicinity of the 100th meridian. Robert Athearn observed that one begins to enter the West at about North Platte, Nebraska, where "towns change, and farming gives way to cattle ranching, the countryside has a drier scent and the horizon takes on a Charlie Russell pastel hue."[2] William Kittredge wrote "the real West started at the long symbolic interstate bridge over that mainline to so many ultimately heart-breaking American versions of heaven, the Missouri River. Out in the middle of South Dakota, I felt myself released into significance. It was clear I was aiming my life in the right direction."[3] In *The Big Rock Candy Mountain*, Stegner wrote,

> At the next service station where he stopped he felt it even stronger, the feeling of belonging, of being in a wellworn and familiar groove. . . . Anything beyond the Missouri was close to home, at least. He was a westerner, whatever that was. The moment he crossed the Big Sioux and got into the brown country where the raw earth showed, the minute the grass got sparser and the air dryer and the service stations less grandiose and the towns rattier, the moment he saw his first lonesome shack on the baking flats with a tipsy windmill creaking away at the reluctant underground water, he knew approximately where he belonged.[4]

One working definition of the American West, then, is the area west of the 100th meridian except Hawaii, which has fundamentally different physical characteristics and a separate set of historical developments. By this standard, the region includes the western parts of the states straddling the 100th meridian (North Dakota, South Dakota, Nebraska, Kansas, Oklahoma, and Texas), the Rocky Mountain states (Montana, Idaho, Wyoming, Colorado, Utah, Nevada, Arizona, and New Mexico), and the Pacific Coast states (Alaska, Washington, Oregon, and California).[5] The special qualities of the American West, however, are more pronounced in some areas within the region than in others. The states along the 100th meridian lack the high percentages of federal public lands that are a key determinant in the West. Even Texas—so archetypically western in some respects—has only a few parcels of public lands, all acquired since statehood.[6] In other parts of the broadly defined region, certain characteristics of the American West also are attenuated. The Pacific Northwest beyond the Cascades, including the Alaska panhandle, has abundant rainfall. California has traditionally shared in the common heritage of the American West; indeed, it has been especially influential, a main platform from which people and ideas have spread throughout the region. During the last generation, however, the coastal area of southern California and the Bay Area farther north have become so heavily urbanized that the traditional regional flavor has been lost to a greater extent than in, say, Salt Lake City, Albuquerque, Phoenix, or Denver. Athearn refused to include the Pacific Coast in his definition of the West.

> [E]qually open to question was the matter of where the West ended. The Pacific Ocean certainly ought to have supplied a definitive stopping point, but here again the West as a state of mind intervened. The Sierra Nevadas and the Cascades curtained off a West Coast people who had developed an economic and cultural empire of their own. They enjoyed greater rainfall, raised different crops than did those who farmed farther east, looked seaward in their thinking, and came to constitute a separate if somewhat provincial society that was more eastern than western, if one accepts the "frontier" as a way of life. . . . [The population of the Pacific Slope] was a modern, urban-oriented, rapidly growing body that had acquired far more quickly those eastern cultural and material characteristics so long envied and mimicked by the newer West. A widely read author . . . called the coastal states the new East and remarked that places such as Portland or Seattle had little about them that was western.[7]

A hard and fast definition of the American West is elusive because the region is molded by so many factors—some concrete, others abstract, some immutable, others dynamic.

Another, less rigidly structured way to think of the American West, then, is to see it as a heartland consisting of the mountain West—the western slopes of the Cascades and the Sierra Nevada east to the eastern slopes of the Rockies—but with strong influence zones reaching out to the 100th meridian and to the Pacific Coast, including Alaska. Further, although the term "American West" connotes territory within the United States, there are a number of instances in which the development of the historical and modern American West is entwined with contiguous areas of Mexico and Canada.

Unique institutions and policies have grown up organically from the land and the people who have inhabited it. Walter Prescott Webb, in his superb book, *The Great Plains* [453], argued that there is an "institutional fault" running down the heart of the nation. This cultural fault line demarcating the eastern edge of the dry country weaves along the 100th and 98th meridians. West of there, Webb concluded, societies created a number of distinctive adaptations to meet the demands of the land. Webb specifically directed his attention to law, detailing the water and federal land disposition laws that were created to meet the needs of the region. We can add many others to Webb's list. In addition to water law and the various homesteading programs, numerous other bodies of policy and law operate solely in the West or apply there in a heavily disproportionate fashion. Subject areas include hardrock mining, federal mineral leasing, American Indians, Spanish and Mexican land grants, Pacific salmon and steelhead, grazing, timber in the national forests, endangered species (especially relating to large mammals such as grizzly bear, wolves, and bighorn sheep), and wilderness. Immigration law and ocean and coastal law might also be included, although they are less distinctly western than the others.

This factor adds a new dimension to regionalism, which we ordinarily associate with history and literature, not with law. Conceptualizations of legal systems within the United States typically rest on the idea that law comes in three layers—

federal, state, and local. In fact, there are at least two major examples of regional bodies of law. One is composed of two centuries of law and policy involving the South's experience with slavery, segregation, and desegregation. The second set of regional laws exists in the American West.

The principles constituting the Law of the American West often seem disconnected and arbitrary if they are studied in a vacuum. These characteristics are particularly noticeable in connection with a phenomenon that pervades policy and law in the West—the dominance of nineteenth-century laws that seem outmoded by today's lights. Some of these laws (water, mining, grazing, and Indian law are perhaps the best examples) may seem outmoded but they are not arbitrary: they arose for good reason out of specific, compelling circumstances. Two leading examples of laissez-faire programs developed to meet the needs of the nineteenth-century West are the prior appropriation doctrine in water law (the "first in time, first in right" rule, allowing water developers a near-unfettered prerogative to divert and dam rivers and granting water users a permanent, vested property right) and the Hardrock Mining Law of 1872 (granting to hardrock miners the right to enter the public domain and, upon discovery of a valuable deposit, to obtain a vested right in the minerals and the overlying 20 acres of land, without payment of any royalty to the United States).[8] Perhaps these and other policies ought to be changed—and a key facet of public policy debate in the West involves exactly that question—but would-be reformers had better be informed to the teeth with an understanding of the historical pressures that created the old laws and the contemporary forces that have kept them in place.

Further, leaving aside the revision of antiquated policies, analysis of the creation of new programs can proceed in a rational, principled way only with a firm understanding of the West's subcultures, traditions, institutions, and natural systems. And one must have a feel for the passion that westerners bring to these issues and for other intangibles, such as what I call the texture of the ground. The furor over, and the ultimate rejection of, the proposal to locate the MX missile system in a vast, sparsely populated area of western Utah and eastern Nevada can be appreciated only through an understanding of the ranch cattle industry, the scarcity of water in the region (130,000 acre-feet would have been required to make concrete shelters for the MX system), the subtle beauty of those high sagebrush plains, and, not inconsequentially, the political might of the Mormon Church. The intensity of the dispute over Indian fishing rights in the Pacific Northwest can be mystifying without a sense of the tenacity with which the tribes cling to hundred-century-old traditional ways; the economic importance of the non-Indian commercial salmon fishing industry; and the near-religious zeal with which hundreds of thousands of sportfishers pursue the region's prime game fish, the steelhead. The fierce and drawn-out legislative campaign to regulate (or protect) "illegal aliens" (or "undocumented workers") must be viewed in the setting of the reliance of western agribusiness on Mexican labor; the fluid, transboundary culture of contemporary Hispanic families; and the open wound caused when the United States tore off the top half of Mexico during the era of Manifest Destiny in the mid-nineteenth century. The pitched battle over federal reserved water rights to instream flows in remote Colorado wilderness areas must be placed in the context of Denver's holy crusade to obtain water, the desperate campaign by western irrigators to protect their first call on western water, the ethereal quality of the backcountry in the high Rockies, and the saga of more than a hundred years of combat over the West's most contested resource.

This book is an attempt to collect some of the writings, fiction as well as nonfiction, that best explain the central forces that have influenced the way of life of the American West. This work also presents a rough organization that, in my view, demonstrates a cohesiveness for the whole region and for the many communities within it. Thus, my approach reflects a judgment that decisionmaking has been conducted in a fragmented way; usually we deal with parts of a larger problem and pretend that the parts are not connected to the whole. This approach has certainly been used in the issue of commodity resources. Traditional western water law, for example, has treated only the consumptive value of water, ignoring wildlife, recreation, and aesthetics. And there are other areas in which we have isolated issues. Questions relating to Alaska, Hispanics, and American Indians, for example, all raise some separate and distinct problems but they also need to be considered as part of the main intellectual bloodstream of the American West; when that approach is not taken, the specialized areas and the greater body both fail to receive valuable nourishment.

An appreciation of the fullness of the region will help create a better society in the West. We need to improve our ability to assess the multifaceted effects of most development decisions (whether the decision is to develop or not to develop) on a wide range of economies, communities, cultures, land forms, watercourses, animals, and intangible values such as beauty and open space. Thus, ultimately, I hope that my groupings will play some role in demonstrating the many legitimate concerns, human and natural, that ought to be given dignity in order to build principled, integrated policy approaches in the American West. To this end, the impressive body of western writing created during the past few decades has made great strides toward identifying the region's constituent parts and their relationship to each other, toward creating a consciousness of the American West as a distinctive place.

The West and the forces that have built its unique institutions are so spread out that a considerable amount of reading is necessary before the bits and pieces even begin to fall together. As a starting dozen, a reader could look to the following, which are not necessarily the best books on the West but which give, in their totality, a spirited and comprehensive sense of historical developments, personalities, cultures, landscapes, and contemporary events. They could logically be read in this order:

Beyond the Hundredth Meridian: John Wesley Powell and the Second Opening of the West by Wallace Stegner [396]; *The Year of Decision: 1846* by Bernard DeVoto [97]; *The Lands No One Knows* by T. H. Watkins and Charles Watson [450]; *The Great Plains* by Walter Prescott Webb [453]; *Angle of Repose*, also by Stegner [400]; *Conservation and the Gospel of Efficiency* by Samuel P. Hays [161]; *Wilderness and the American Mind* by Roderick Nash [299]; *Coming into the Country* by John McPhee [269]; *Custer Died for Your Sins* by Vine Deloria, Jr. [95]; *Cadillac Desert* by Marc Reisner [343]; *The Milagro Beanfield War* by John Nichols [306]; and *Basin and Range*, also by McPhee [270]. To make it a baker's dozen, and to guarantee the reader's outrage (different brands of outrage for different readers), one could include *The Monkey Wrench Gang* by Edward Abbey [4]. Another irresistible entry— although it focuses somewhat more on the upper Midwest rather than the West—is Aldo Leopold's *A Sand County Almanac* [232], perhaps the greatest work on conservation ever written. One also ought to subscribe to the award-winning newspaper of the West, the bimonthly *High Country News* [170], published in Paonia, Colorado. But those fine sources are just a beginning, and students of the region will want to proceed with many of the additional works that are discussed throughout this book.

NOTES

1. Stegner, *The Sound of Mountain Water*, p. 33 [399].
2. Athearn, *The Mythic West in Twentieth-Century America*, p. 18 [21].
3. Kittredge, *Owning It All: Essays*, pp. 66–67 [214].
4. Stegner, *The Big Rock Candy Mountain*, pp. 463–464 [395].
5. The West is also sometimes defined as the eleven western states or the seventeen western states (which would include all land within the six states along the 100th meridian). Both categories exclude Alaska, an omission I cannot accept. "The Last Frontier" is more than a handy tourist slogan: western attitudes, natural wonders, stresses, and policies flourish in Alaska at least as heart-

ily as in any of the contiguous western states.

6. All other western states were carved out of the public domain and most land remained federal after statehood, but Texas obtained title to nonprivate land within state boundaries. Texas was able to achieve that result because it came to the statehood negotiations as an independent republic owning most of the land within its boundaries, rather than as a federally created territory.

7. Athearn, supra, p. 19 [21].

8. For the historical development of those programs, see generally Dunbar, *Forging New Rights in Western Waters* [109]; Leshy, *The Mining Law: A Study in Perpetual Motion* [233]. For a collection of essays on the legal history of the American West, see "Law in the West" in *Journal of the West* [195]. See also Bakken, *The Development of Law on the Rocky Mountain Frontier, 1850–1912* [24].

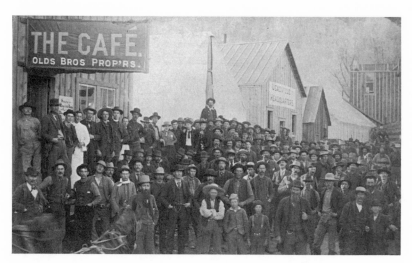

June 8, 1892, Creede, Colorado, two years after Creede's spectacular silver rush and five minutes after Bob Ford, the "slayer of Jesse James," was killed in his own saloon (the white tent in the middle background). *Courtesy, Colorado Historical Society.*

2

THE EVENTS

No one book encompasses the history of the American West. The geography is too varied and the events too numerous for one canvas. There are several standard sources. The Turner thesis on the closing of the frontier in the late nineteenth century [429] is a classic. Turner's work is examined by Hofstadter and Lipset, in *Turner and the Sociology of the Frontier* [173]. Ray Allen Billington's book, *Westward Expansion* [39], provides a detailed text that has great structural clarity.

The Turner-Billington approach, however, ultimately is incomplete because of its rigidity in fixing 1890—the supposed close of the frontier—as the determinative moment in western history. In fact, the history of the American West is far better understood in terms of continuity, of the deep-rooted influence of nineteenth-century events on a pluralistic modern society. Turner's pronouncement that the frontier was closed was premised on a finding in the 1890 census that population in the West had reached the figure of at least two persons per square mile and that "there can hardly be said to be a frontier line."[1] Such reasoning might well have reflected the view from Cambridge, but it would surely have seemed curious, for example, in late nineteenth-century Nevada, where the population lay mainly in a thin fringe along the western border; in Montana, Idaho, and Wyoming, all of which were real outposts even though they managed to achieve statehood in 1889 or 1890; in Utah, which remained in territorial status until 1896; or in Arizona and New Mexico, which were not admitted into the Union until 1912. Wallace Stegner is quite certain that the Saskatchewan and Montana country that he lived in as a boy in the 1910s was still a frontier. See Stegner, *Wolf Willow* [397]. Further, the frontier thesis falls short of giving full coverage to the West. It offers little insight into Indian country, Hispanics in the United States–Mexico borderland, Mormon country, or the place of women in the westward expansion. And the thesis does not even purport to encompass Alaska.

I am far more persuaded by scholars such as Patricia Nelson Limerick: "Let the car break down in the desert, or let the Indians file a lawsuit to reassert an old land claim and . . . the frontier is suddenly reopened. Frontier [as viewed by Turner and Billington] is an unsubtle concept in a subtle world."[2] Limerick's brightly written book, *Legacy of Conquest* [239], is masterful. It blends the old, the new, the land, and the subcultures of the American West and, to my eye at least, finally disproves the usefulness of the frontier thesis as the lens through which to view western history. Of course, Turner and Billington have many valuable things to say about the frontier and its impact on the human spirit and imagination; of course, they remain basic sources; of course, they ought to be read— and with real care and respect. But the West is, and always has been, too variegated to be reduced to any single formula.[3]

There are other books that cover broad aspects of western history. In *Virgin Land: The American West as Symbol and Myth* [385], an intellectual history of the region, Henry Nash Smith explores the many different myths—whether bred of romance, avarice, or ignorance—that have shaped the development of the West. Dana and Fairfax, in *Forest and Range Policy* [88], give a short, interpretive account of federal public land policy. Paul Gates's study, *History of Public Land Law Development* [138], is comprehensive on most issues in that field (it slights recreation and wilderness), but it is more of a reference tool than a readable history. More recently, the high level of interest in the West has been exemplified by several histories on various aspects of western resource policy, most of them sharply critical of what the authors view as the exploitative policies of the past and present.[4]

These sources will help in fitting the puzzle together, but ultimately a reader will find it best to grasp western history by looking at subregions, eras, movements, and personalities. In this chapter, and elsewhere in this book, I sometimes use metaphors—examples include Hoover Dam, the Mussel Slough Tragedy, and the Johnson County War—that are important in their own right but also symbolize broader developments. For comprehensive bibliographies of western history, see Malone [482], Nichols [483], and Tuska and Piekarski [486] which discusses films as well as books.

The Turning Points

The California Gold Rush   To be sure, the history of the West hardly began in 1848. Indian people had lived in the region for thousands of years, Spanish missions had been settled as early as the sixteenth century, the Louisiana Purchase of 1803 had laid the groundwork for the westward movement, the fur trappers had made explorations west of the Continental Divide, and the Oregon and California trails had brought settlers west. On the overland passages, see Parkman, *The Oregon Trail* [316]; Reid, *Law for the Elephant: Property and Social Behavior on the Overland Trail* [342]; and A. B. Guthrie, Jr.'s novel, *The Way West* [148]. The ferment in the region as of the mid-1840s, including the Bear Flag Revolt in California and the Mormon migration to Utah, is told well in Bernard DeVoto's, *The Year of Decision: 1846* [97], which is the final installment in DeVoto's trilogy. DeVoto covers earlier eras in *The Course of Empire* [99] and *Across the Wide Missouri* [98]. Richard Henry Dana's account of his visit to California in 1834, *Two Years Before the Mast* [87], is a classic.

But the course of events was dramatically accelerated and expanded by the chain reaction set off by James Marshall's discovery of gold on January 24, 1848, at Sutter's Mill on the American River not far from Sacramento. The leading work on the Gold Rush is the careful, straightforward history by Rodman Paul, *California Gold* [318], which analyzes the effects of this movement that apparently was the largest migration of human beings in world history. Other outstanding accounts include Holliday, *The World Rushed In: The California Gold Rush Experience* [175] and Robert Lewis Taylor's *The Travels of Jaimie McPheeters*, the rollicking saga of two forty-niners, a 14-year-old boy, and his enthusiastic but star-crossed father [420]. Population radiated from the California gold country as finds were made in Nevada, Oregon, Alaska, and most other western states.

A much-acclaimed, first-hand sketch of the early California mining camps is by Louise Amelia Knapp Smith Clappe, under the nom de plume "Dame Shirley," who wrote letters from Rich Bar on the Feather River to her sister back east [67]. *The Shirley Letters* are an accurate and detailed, yet inevitably colorful, description of life in the mining camps during this remarkable time. The small, independent miner tended to have a brief moment in the sun before mining turned corporate (see Lingenfelter, [240]), but the region continued to be spectacularly wild and woolly, as reflected in Mark Twain's luscious *Roughing It* [432]. Other important works are Paul's *Mining Frontiers of the Far West, 1848–1880* [319] and Greever's *The Bonanza West: The Story of the Western Mining Rushes, 1848–1900* [145]. The Gold Rush produced several people of stature, including Supreme Court Justice Stephen J. Field. See, for example, Swisher, *Stephen J. Field: Craftsman of the Law* [417]. Senator William Stewart of Nevada, who led the way for the Hardrock Mining Law of 1872, wrote an appropriately boisterous, if not always

16

believable, autobiography covering his two generations in public life [411]. For another autobiography by a leading congressional figure involved in mining issues, see Julian, *Political Recollections, 1840 to 1872* [196].

The Opening of the Public Domain   For most of the 1800s, there was virtually no federal restraint on private uses of public land and resources. The public domain (the vast majority of all land in the West) was simply left open for ranching, mining, homesteading, water diversions, and hunting and fishing. Beginning in the late nineteenth century, the national forests and national parks were set aside and put under management, but no such action was taken with respect to the remaining hundreds of millions of acres of public domain until the Taylor Grazing Act was passed in 1934.

The results were mixed. The homesteading policy, as novels by Hamlin Garland, *A Son of the Middle Border* [136], *A Daughter of the Middle Border* [137], and O.E. Rölvaag, *Giants in the Earth* [352], showed so well, was a bitterly frustrating, dirt-in-your-teeth, wind-in-your-face challenge to honest, individual westering people. The struggle continued well into this century when, as vividly portrayed by John Steinbeck, *The Grapes of Wrath* [407], *East of Eden* [409], *Cannery Row* [408], *Tortilla Flat* [405], *Of Mice and Men* [406], and Woody Guthrie, *Bound for Glory* [149], the Dust Bowl of the early 1930s drove farmers and workers west to California. See also Lange and Taylor, *An American Exodus: A Record of Human Erosion* [221] (with Dorothea Lange's wonderful photographs). To those not so honest, the federal land laws were the sturdy levers by which ragtag migrants and future magnates pried loose uncountable tens of millions of acres of land from public ownership through a kaleidoscopic array of fraudulent schemes. For a careful survey, and an exhaustive bibliography, of this blend of frontier ingenuity and criminal conduct, see Dick, *The Lure of the Land: A Social History of the Public Lands from the Articles of Confederation to the New Deal* [101]. For joyous reading, see Puter, *Looters of the Public Domain*

[338], written by an expert, the self-styled "king of the Oregon land fraud ring," while serving time in prison.

The hands-off federal policy toward the majority of all western land has left us with, among other things, an overgrazed range, extraordinary soil erosion problems, outmoded classes of rights, and an inefficient, checkerboard, land-ownership pattern across the rural West. On the other hand, the homesteaders program held out hope to little people: it was one of the most progressive land distribution policies ever undertaken by any nation. Walter Prescott Webb, writing in 1931, called the ranch cattle industry "perhaps the most . . . distinctive institution that America has produced."[5]

Two major pieces, Louise Peffer's *The Closing of the Public Domain* [321] and Philip Foss's *Politics and Grass* [132], examine the opening and closing of the public rangelands. They are the kind of full, sensibly presented treatments that both bind together specific historical movements and draw out general lessons. A different but equally valuable source is *The Lands No One Knows*, [450] coauthored by T. H. Watkins, a stellar wordscraftsman with a fine knowledge of the West, and Charles Watson, a former Bureau of Land Management employee with twenty-some-odd years of card files and inside knowledge. The result is a lusty, irreverent exposé of the "Two Gun Desmonds" who captured public domain policy. Some academics may frown at this colorful piece, but there *were* Two Gun Desmonds and it is probably best that their story be told with élan, as is the case with *The Lands No One Knows*.

The Creation of Yellowstone National Park

In 1872, Congress set aside the fabulous high plateau in the northern Rockies as a "pleasuring-ground for the benefit and enjoyment of the people." The creation of Yellowstone National Park is a monument in western history for a number of reasons. The permanent protection of this exquisite land of cauldrons, lakes, and headwaters is important in its own right (see Chapter 4 for sources on the Greater Yellowstone Ecosystem). In addition,

Yellowstone was this country's (and the world's) first national park and, as such, became a model for the modern national park system.[6]

In an even broader sense, Yellowstone symbolizes the beginnings of an important set of new ideas in the American West. As Roderick Nash shows in his leading work on preservation history and theory, *Wilderness and the American Mind* [299], there were other early stirrings of preservation policy. See also Sax [366]. Still, the creation of Yellowstone is the most fitting milestone. In the heart of an era of exploitation of the West's natural resources, Yellowstone signaled very different kinds of aspirations that would come front and center in years to come.

Indian Allotment   By about 1880, homesteaders, ranchers, timber companies, miners, and other settlers came to see Indian reservations as a major obstacle to westward expansion. The Dawes General Allotment Act of 1887 allowed the transmutation of tribally owned lands into individual parcels, or allotments. Great amounts of these allotted lands were sold to non-Indians or lost at tax sales. The 1887 act also authorized large areas of some reservations to be designated as "surplus" to tribal needs; such lands were then added to the public domain for disposition. Allotment helped open the West for settlement by non-Indians, but it was devastating to Indian interests. In all, the total Indian land estate dropped from 140 million acres in 1887 to 50 million acres by 1934, thus transferring about 5 percent of all land in the lower forty-eight states to non-Indian settlers and corporations.

Two fine studies, Francis Paul Prucha's *American Indian Policy in Crisis* [332][7] and Frederick Hoxie's *A Final Promise* [180], treat this major set of developments, analyzing the allotment program as well as other aspects of assimilationist policy, such as the creation of the federal Indian boarding schools and the work of Christian missionaries. For other leading accounts of this era, see Kinney, *A Continent Lost, A Civilization Won: Indian Land Tenure in America* [211]; Otis, *The Dawes Act and the Allot-*

19

ment of Indian Land [314]; Fritz, *The Movement for Indian Assimilation, 1860 to 1890* [135]; Mary Young, *Redskins, Ruffleshirts, and Rednecks: Indian Allotments in Alabama and Mississippi: 1830–1860* [475]. The ambiguities at play during this period, as in other eras of federal Indian policy, are evident in a collection of essays edited by Father Prucha, written by the "Friends of the Indian" [337], who generally favored allotment as the best option for the tribes.

The Construction of Hoover Dam   After private and state efforts to fund large water projects had proved inadequate, Congress enacted reclamation legislation in 1902, thus assuring federal funding for big-scale western water development. Although the dam-building program was active from the beginning, allowing millions of acres of land to be opened for irrigated agriculture, the largest projects were not completed until the 1930s and later, with the construction of such giant dams as Hoover and Glen Canyon on the Colorado, Shasta on the Sacramento, and Grand Coulee and Bonneville on the Columbia. Reclamation helped remake the West. No governmental program has mattered more to the region.

Wallace Stegner's *Beyond the Hundredth Meridian* [396] tells the story of the visionary John Wesley Powell, who understood aridity and its key role in the West. This is a great book—perhaps the very first that one should read to learn of the region. *Hail Columbia* [415] is an account by a devout New Dealer who believed in the big dams. John McPhee's *Encounters with the Archdruid* [268] relates a raft trip down the Colorado River and the heated discussions between David Brower, the dynamic executive director of the Sierra Club, and Floyd Dominy, the resourceful reclamation commissioner. Robert Dunbar, a historian, has written a solid account of the development of western water law [109]. For an understanding of the idealism and spirit of the early reclamation movement, see Smythe, *The Conquest of Arid America* [386].

I use Hoover Dam as the metaphor for the reclamation

program because it was the first of the really big dams. Wiley and Gottlieb, in *Empires in the Sun* [461], identify Hoover Dam's pivotal role in the West and recount the formation of the "six companies" (including Bechtel, Kaiser, and Utah International) that, with financing from the young Bank of America, were in charge of construction. Philip Fradkin's *A River No More* [134] is a splendid examination of water policy in the Colorado River basin and serves as a primer on western resources in general. *Cadillac Desert* [343] by Marc Reisner is a powerful attack on the subsidy-ridden, overbuilt system of western water development and has reached a broad audience. Donald Worster's *Rivers of Empire* [471] is an extraordinarily ambitious venture that sees the dam-building boom as having created a "hydraulic society" in the desert—a society doomed to crumble under its own weight. Worster may try to prove too much—the crumbling is not nearly as certain for me as it is for Worster, nor the hats quite as black as he paints them—but the book is valuable reading. Fradkin, Reisner, and Worster all contain bibliographies on the transcendent matter of water development—a core issue one must have in hand to understand the American West.

The Post–World War II Boom   Except for a few population centers on the Pacific Coast, the American West was mostly a backwater area as World War II drew to a close. A major segment of the region's history has occurred since. Jet planes and the interstate highway system made the West accessible to easterners seeking recreation or permanent residence. The population explosion after the war created a demand for housing that the government sought to meet by sharply increased timber sales from the old-growth stands in the national forests of Oregon, Washington, and southeast Alaska. The climate of the Sun Belt of the Southwest drew population in droves. The powder snow and winter sun in the Rockies generated the construction of the largest ski resorts in the nation, which have been magnets for winter visitors from all over the world. The uranium boom of the 1950s and, to a much greater extent, the energy boom of the 1970s remade cities such as Denver, Salt Lake City, Anchorage, Casper, and Billings; when the energy boom tailed off in the 1980s, it raised the specter of yet another "boom and bust" cycle. As noted in Chapter 1, urbanization wrought deep changes, especially on the West Coast.

The arrival of the post-war immigrants and the stresses on the land and its people have been the subject of an increasing stream of books on the new West (see, for example, the sources given in note 4 in this chapter). Gerald D. Nash, in *The American West Transformed* [298], sees World War II as the watershed and examines the resulting changes in the eleven western states. Former Colorado Governor Dick Lamm collaborated with Michael McCarthy on *The Angry West* [220], which deals with modern developments quite comprehensively. They argue that the West has been "colonized" by interests outside of the region. An especially thoughtful and personal statement is the posthumously published *The Mythic West in Twentieth-Century America* [21] by leading historian Robert Athearn, who looks at the ways in which the old West lives on in the new West.

The Epic Conflicts

Conquest by Manifest Destiny The phrase Manifest Destiny, coined during the Polk administration, 1845 through 1849, aptly describes the quasi-religious righteousness of U.S. policy in the American West during the nineteenth and early twentieth centuries. Manifest Destiny operated to impose control both over peoples, most notably American Indians and Hispanics, and over natural resources. The consequences remain with us and are at the heart of the "legacy of conquest" described by historian Patricia Nelson Limerick [239].

Often violent Indian-white conflicts led to the settlement of Indian tribes on reservations, allowing the westward movement to proceed. The literature is extensive but necessarily

22

diffuse because several hundred tribes were involved. Father Prucha, in addition to his treatise on federal Indian policy [335] [336], has produced two bibliographies [333][334]. Historians have focused a great deal of attention on Andrew Jackson's removal program that led to the Trail of Tears of the 1830s, whereby federal troops forcibly marched the so-called Five Civilized Tribes from their aboriginal lands in the southeast to what is now Oklahoma. See Foreman, *Indian Removal: The Emigration of the Five Civilized Tribes of Indians* [131]; Debo, *The Rise and Fall of the Choctaw Republic* [93]; Debo, *The Road to Disappearance: A History of the Creek Indians* [92]. Congress continued the policy in later decades, when more than 100 tribal groups were moved to Oklahoma. Alvin Josephy's *The Nez Perce Indians and the Opening of the Northwest* [194] deals with just one tribe and its heroic leader, Chief Joseph, but this masterful work helps build a broader understanding of the forces that led to the creation of the reservation system. Robert Trennert, in *Alternative to Extinction* [426], concludes that the reservations actually may have served to benefit the tribes by insulating them from white aggressiveness. Helen Hunt Jackson's classic, *A Century of Dishonor* [189], recounts the despair that had enveloped Indian country by the late nineteenth century.

For most people, Manifest Destiny is an abstraction, except perhaps as it relates to American Indians. Hispanics, however, were affected in many of the same ways. In 1845, during President Polk's tenure, the United States annexed Texas, then an independent republic. The Mexican-American War, for which there was no clear cause except U.S. expansionist fervor, culminated in the Treaty of Guadalupe Hidalgo in 1848, in which the United States forced Mexico to cede California, Nevada, Utah, most of Arizona, and parts of New Mexico, Colorado, and Wyoming. In all, the territory of the Republic of Mexico was cut nearly in half. See Weber, *The Mexican Frontier, 1821–1846: The American Southwest Under Mexico* [454]; Brack, *Mexico Views Manifest Destiny, 1821–1846: An Essay on the Origins of the Mexican War* [42]; Bauer, *The Mexican War (1846–1848)*

[28]. The 1848 treaty purported to respect prior Spanish and Mexican land grants, but federal laws and American enterprise managed to separate Hispanics in California and the Southwest from most of their land. See Weber, *Foreigners in Their Native Land: Historical Roots of the Mexican Americans* [455]. For a biography of one of the principal beneficiaries of the land title process, see Westphall, *Thomas Benton Catron and His Era* [459]. The new, arbitrary international border separated family from family and remains the geographical manifestation of an immigration policy that is satisfactory to almost no one—American farmers, federal officials, or Hispanics in (or seeking to migrate to) their former homeland. See McWilliams, *North from Mexico: The Spanish Speaking People of the United States* [273]; Kiser and Kiser, *Mexican Workers in the United States: Historical and Political Perspectives* [212]. See also Cafferty and McReady [53], and Paz [320]. Valk has compiled a comprehensive bibliography on the United States–Mexico borderlands [487].

The Mussel Slough Tragedy   The railroads became transcontinental in 1869 when the golden spike was driven at Promontory Point in Utah where the Central Pacific and Union Pacific lines met. This event created the transportation link that finally made the Pacific Coast readily accessible to easterners. As part of the bargain, Congress transferred to the railroads some 120 million acres of land along the routes—an area as large as California and half of Washington combined. The railroad grants continue to influence western life because of the resultant concentration of wealth by the railroads and their holding companies and because of the various inconveniences caused by the checkerboard land pattern created by the railroad land grants; whether the grants needed to be so extravagant has long been a point of sharp debate. Several articles on the railroad land grants are excerpted in the helpful anthology edited by Carstensen, *The Public Lands: Studies in the History of the Public Domain* [59].

The Mussel Slough tragedy took place in 1880 in the southern

San Joaquin Valley. Farmers had settled on railroad grant lands, but a dispute arose between the railroads and the farmers over the sale terms. The settlers refused to move out. In a shoot-out with law enforcement officers, seven settlers were killed. The incident is described in a short book on the subject by J. L. Brown [50] and in Oscar Lewis's *The Big Four* [234].

Mussel Slough has also attracted fiction writers. Frank Norris used the incident as the climax of his major novel, *The Octopus* [311]. Near the end of the book, Norris presents an encounter between Presley, the idealistic young protagonist, and Shelgrim, president of the P. & S.W. Railroad—Shelgrim surely being modeled after Collis P. Huntington, president of the Southern Pacific and one of Oscar Lewis's Big Four. The dialogue in Shelgrim's office in San Francisco is one of the great moments in the literature of the West. After all of the sorrow in the valley, Presley is told in no uncertain terms of the inevitability of progress.

> "Believe this, young man," exclaimed Shelgrim, laying a thick, powerful forefinger on the table to emphasize his words, "try to believe this—to begin with—*that railroads build themselves.* Where there is a demand sooner or later there will be a supply. Mr. Derrick, does he grow his wheat? The Wheat grows itself. What does he count for? Does he supply the force? What do I count for? Do I build the railroad? You are dealing with forces, young man, when you speak of Wheat and the Railroads, not with men. There is the Wheat, the supply. It must be carried to feed the People. There is the demand. The Wheat is one force, the Railroad another, and there is the law that governs them— supply and demand. Men have only little to do in the whole business. Complications may arise, conditions that bear hard on the individual—crush him maybe—*but the Wheat will be carried to feed the people* as inevitably as it will grow. If you want to fasten the blame of the affair at Los Muertos on any one person, you will make a mistake. Blame conditions, not men."[8]

The Johnson County War One by-product of leaving the public domain as a commons, open for the taking, was the long string of violent disputes among cattle ranchers, sheepherders, and homesteaders. The most famous of these conflicts was the Johnson County War of April 1892 in northeastern Wyoming. Homesteaders moved in, under the public land laws, to settle federal lands grazed by cattlemen exercising customary range rights. Threats were issued to the settlers, who were then accused of retaliation by means of cattle rustling. The ranchers brought in 52 "regulators" from out of state to shoot down the homesteaders. Two people were killed and ranch property was set afire, but an ultimate showdown—dynamite was about to be employed—was averted by the arrival of federal troops.

The Johnson County War is the subject of Helena Huntington Smith's *The War on Powder River* [384]. For a colorful, pro-homesteader account, see Mercer, *The Banditti of the Plains* [275]. See also Owen Wister's prototype of the western novel, *The Virginian: A Horseman of the Plains* [468]. Like Mussel Slough, the incident has been fictionalized. See McPherren, *Trail's End* [272], and Elston, *The Marked Men* [115]. Harry Drago treats the west-wide phenomenon of range conflicts in *The Great Range Wars* [108]. Larry McMurtry overstates the level of violence during this era, but his novel, *Lonesome Dove* [265], is an unforgettable plains odyssey stretching from Mexico to Canada.

Water for Los Angeles   The growth of the largest city in the nation depended on importing water to arid southern California. At the turn of the century, Los Angeles embarked on a crusade that would transport water from the Trinity and Feather rivers in northern California; from the Colorado River on the Arizona border; from the Owens River some 200 miles to the northeast, on the east side of the Sierra Nevada; and from the Mono Lake basin, north of the Owens Valley.

Los Angeles's reach up into Owens Valley and Mono Lake crippled the local economy and inflamed passions that led to various dynamitings of the aqueduct and, even today, to continuing rounds of litigation and the deployment of an occasional Molotov cocktail in the Bishop offices of the Los

Angeles Department of Water and Power. The shenanigans, fraud, tenacity, and municipal planning employed by the big city are set out in *Water and Power* by William Kahrl [197]. Remi Nadeau's *The Water Seekers* [297] is the other leading piece on the Los Angeles–Owens Valley controversy, which is treated in most of the books on west-wide water policy (see, for example, Reisner [343] and Worster [471]). See also Hoffman, *Vision or Villainy: Origins of the Owens Valley–Los Angeles Water Controversy* [172].

Hetch Hetchy Many of the epic environmental disputes in the West have involved the construction of dams that flood deep canyons, valuable both for their beauty and their storage capacity. The first such conflict, and still one of the most noteworthy, was the flooding (in 1913) of Hetch Hetchy, a magnificent valley north of Yosemite in the Sierra Nevada, in order to secure water for San Francisco. The dispute was a collision between leading figures of the time—John Muir and the Sierra Club, on the one side, and Teddy Roosevelt and Gifford Pinchot, on the other. The completion of the Hetch Hetchy project may well have led to the despondent Muir's death in 1914, but it contributed mightily to some of Muir's objectives, including the creation of the National Park Service in 1916. See Jones, *John Muir and the Sierra Club: The Battle for Yosemite* [192], and Richardson, "The Struggle for the Valley: California's Hetch Hetchy Controversy 1905–1913" [345].

Other controversies over western dams have stirred deep passions. In the mid-1950s, the Dalles Dam on the Columbia River flooded the historic latticework of Indian fishing platforms at Celilo Falls, one of the great salmon fishing sites in the world. Chief, in Ken Kesey's *One Flew Over the Cuckoo's Nest* [207], was a Celilo Falls Indian, and Kesey's masterpiece has long and poignant passages about the inundation. The modern environmental movement cut its teeth on another proposal of the 1950s. A dam at Echo Park on the Green River would have backed water into Dinosaur National Monument on the Colorado–Utah border. Opponents marshaled new forces and defeated the dam at Echo Park, but the compromise allowed the flooding of Glen Canyon on the Colorado River. See, for example, Richardson, *Dams, Parks & Politics* [346], and Nash [299].

Alaska Land Alaska contains 365 million acres stretching from the Aleutian Islands in the west to the rain forests of the panhandle in the east—an east-west reach equal to the distance between California and Florida. The land area exceeds the combined acreage of California, Oregon, Washington, Idaho, and Montana. All of the age-old pressures over land and resources in the Lower Forty-eight have been magnified several times over in Alaska.

Alaska achieved statehood in 1959 and bargained for the transfer to the state of 103 million acres of federal land, by far the greatest amount obtained by any state. U.S. Senator Ernest Gruening has rendered his firsthand version in *The Battle for Alaska Statehood* [146], a colorful, pro-development piece that gives the flavor of the times. The standard scholarly account is by Claus Naske [300].

Even when statehood was granted to Alaska, the United States never resolved the land claims of Alaska Natives, who objected to surveys conducted by the state and, later, to exploration in connection with the discovery of oil at Prudhoe Bay in 1968. The legal result was the Alaska Native Claims Settlement Act (ANCSA) of 1971, which provided for the selection of an additional 44 million acres by the natives. Mary Berry has written an account of the high-stakes conflicts and coalitions leading to the passage of ANCSA and the building of the Alaska pipeline to carry petroleum south from Prudhoe Bay, the site of the largest producing oil field in U.S. history [36]. See also Arnold, *Alaska Native Land Claims* [20]. The politics of the 1971 act also allowed environmentalists to become main players in Alaska land distribution, the result being the Alaska National Interest Lands Conservation Act of 1980, one of the major natural resources statutes ever adopted. See, for example, Cahn, *The Fight to Save Wild Alaska* (1982) [54], and "Alaska National Interest Lands," in *Alaska Geographic* [7].

Land and resource issues continue to boil in Alaska. John McPhee's outstanding portrait of the state as of the mid-1970s, *Coming into the Country* [269], captures attitudes and pressures that will persist for the foreseeable future. Thomas Berger, Canadian judge and scholar, conducted a two-year, foundation-supported series of hearings in Native villages in the style of a Canadian commission. His report, *Village Journey* [32], is a beautifully crafted analysis, with recommendations, of the issues relating to Native land and political rights that continue to be matters of front-line importance in Alaska.

NOTES

1. Turner, *The Frontier in American History*, p. 1 [429].
2. Limerick, *Legacy of Conquest: The Unbroken Past of the American West*, p. 25 [239].
3. I have had my own internal struggle with *Legacy of Conquest*: the temptation has been great to list it among my "first dozen" books on the American West. My reason for not doing so is simply an innate reluctance to make such a sweeping judgment on a book that I have not lived with for a while. In any event, readers will surely find Limerick's book to be enormously provocative and insightful. For another recent piece critical of the Turner thesis, see Slotkin, *The Fatal Environment: The Myth of the Frontier in the Age of Industrialization, 1800–1890* [381].
4. For example, see Reisner, *Cadillac Desert: The American West and Its Disappearing Water* [343]; Fradkin, *A River No More: The Colorado River and the West* [134]; Wiley and Gottlieb, *Empires in the Sun: The Rise of the New AmericanWest* [461]; Zaslowsky and the Wilderness Society, *These American Lands: Parks, Wilderness, and the Public Lands* [477]; Leshy, *The Mining Law: A Study in Perpetual Motion* [233]; Wyant, *Westward in Eden: The Public Lands and the Conservation Movement* [474]; Shanks, *This Land Is Your Land: The Struggle to Save America's Public Lands* [374]; Lamm and McCarthy, *The Angry*

West: A Vulnerable Land and Its Future [220]; Worster, *Rivers of Empire: Water, Aridity, and the Growth of the American West* [471]; Brown and Ingram, *Water and Poverty in the Southwest* [49]; Turner, *Beyond Geography: The Western Spirit Against the Wilderness* [430].

5. See Webb, *The Great Plains*, p. 224 [453].

6. There has been somewhat less written about the national park system than one might expect. Park policy is treated ably in Runte, *National Parks: The American Experience* [356]. The standard history is Ise, *Our National Parks Policy—A Critical History* [187], which is more descriptive than analytical. For a solid biography of the first National Park Service director, see Shankland, *Steve Mather of the National Parks* [373]. For reflections by the second director, Horace Albright, see Albright, *The Birth of the National Park Service: The Founding Years* [11]. For useful histories of individual parks, see, for example, Haines, *The Yellowstone Story* [154]; Righter, *Crucible for Conservation: The Creation of Grand Teton National Park* [347]; Buchholtz, *Rocky Mountain National Park: A History* [52]. The excellent study by Joseph Sax, *Mountains Without Handrails: Reflections on the National Parks* [366], is about the wilderness ideal rather than the parks per se.

7. Father Prucha has also written the definitive history on federal Indian policy. See Prucha, *The Great Father: The United States Government and the American Indians* (two volumes) [335]. *The Great Father* is now available in an abridged, paperback edition [336]. Prucha has also published two bibliographies of federal Indian policy. One is quite short and excellent for the beginning reader [334], while the other is exhaustive [333]. For short histories of Indian affairs, see Washburn, *The Indian in America* [443]; Dippie, *The Vanishing American: White Attitudes and U.S. Indian Policy* [102].

8. Norris, *The Octopus*, p. 405 [311]. For another fictionalized account of Mussell Slough, See Miller, *First the Blade* [277].

Woman and child in a field of dry grown Red Cross and Turkey Red wheat; New Castle, Wyoming. 1908, by J. E. Stimson. *Courtesy, Wyoming State Archives, Museums and Historical Department.*

THE PEOPLE

The Leaders

Lewis and Clark and the Mountain Men   Jefferson's decision to explore the Louisiana Purchase and to find a land route to the Pacific Coast punctuated the young nation's determination to claim the West. Meriwether Lewis and William Clark headed the expedition of 1803–1805 that, then as now, captured the public imagination. The Lewis and Clark journals have been condensed by Bernard DeVoto, who added his own commentary [100]. In addition, the journals have been reprinted in full by Arno Press, the publishing service of the *New York Times*, with an introduction by DeVoto. See Thwaites, *Original Journals of the Lewis & Clark Expedition* [423]. Another standard source is by Bakeless [22], and Washington Irving's *Astoria* [186] offers an account of the era. See also Irving, *The Adventures of Captain Bonneville, U.S.A., in the Rocky Mountains and the Far West* [185]. Gary Holthaus's inspired collection of poetry, *Circling Back* [176], is based on journals of the early West, including those of Lewis and Clark.

Perhaps no aspect of western history has elicited the rich and extensive attention given to the mountain men. White explorers had gone west before 1822, but a brightly drawn, although brief, era dawned on February 13 of that year when William Henry Ashley advertised in the *Missouri Gazette & Public Advertiser* to engage "ONE HUNDRED MEN, to ascend the river Missouri to its source, there to be employed for one, two or three years." A photocopy of this famous advertisement is reproduced in the handsome collection by Morgan, *The West of William H. Ashley, 1822–1838* [280]. Robert Glass Cleland's *This Reckless Breed of Men* [72] and DeVoto's *Across the Wide Missouri* [98] are both sparkling, reliable sources on this colorful time, which began to tail off in 1836 when felt hats went out of favor in Paris and the demand for beaver pelts plummeted. See also Don Berry, *A Majority of Scoundrels: An Informal History of the Rocky Mountain Fur Company* [34] and David Lavender, *Bent's Fort* [223], and *The Rockies* [224]. Numerous biographies have been written on these rough-hewn wilderness heroes.[1] The best is Dale Morgan's work, *Jedediah Smith and the Opening of the West* [279], which examines the life of the intrepid Smith, who among many other things led the first recorded crossing of the Sierra Nevada (made, by the way, from west to east); it also affords a solid understanding of the fur trade in general. A. B. Guthrie, Jr.'s *The Big Sky* [147] is a widely praised novel on the mountain men. Another fine work, *The Mountain Men* [303] by John Neihardt, is presented in the form of three heroic songs. *Trask* [33] by Don Berry deals with the Oregon coast in 1848, but it also catches the spirit of the mountain men. See also Berry, *Moontrap* [35].

The Big Four The Gilded Age of the nineteenth century fostered the creation of many personal empires but none more extensive than those of the Big Four of the Southern Pacific Railroad, all of whose names still adorn financial, educational, and philanthropic institutions in California: Collis P. Huntington, Leland Stanford, Mark Hopkins, and Charles Crocker. See Lewis, *The Big Four* [234]. The era also produced such magnates as Henry Miller, the cattle king [424]; Marcus Daly,

William A. Clark, and F. S. Heinze of the Butte copper mines [142]; Thomas B. Catron, a lawyer who built an estate in excess of 3 million acres from the New Mexico land claims process [459]; and William Ralston, a San Francisco banker who made a fortune out of Nevada's Comstock Lode before his fall. See Lyman, *The Saga of the Comstock Lode: Boom Days in Virginia City* [250]; Lyman, *Ralston's Ring: California Plunders the Comstock Lode* [251]; and Lewis and Hall, *Bonanza Inn* [235]. All of these men, and others of their ilk, helped build the West's economy. They also contributed directly to the Law of the American West both by making laws to suit their interests and by serving as symbols of the need for reform because of their perceived excesses.

John Wesley Powell   Powell properly can be called a visionary because he so clearly identified the significance of aridity in the future of the West. He explained the constraints on society that aridity made mandatory, saw how policy needed to be tailored because of the lack of precipitation, and had the courage to confront the expansionists with the unpopular fact that western resources were finite. Stegner's great biography of Powell is standard reading [396]. Powell's own reports—recounting his exploration of the Colorado River in 1869 and setting out his recommendations on water and land policy to Congress—deserve to be read in their original form [329][330].

John Muir   Muir's writing and advocacy injected preservationist theory into mainstream western resources policy. Muir—named the single greatest Californian in history in a 1976 California Historical Society poll—succeeded in celebrating and communicating wildness, with all of its majesty and unruliness, in ways that cut to the soul: climbing to the top of a high Sierra fir tree during a storm and being "flapped and swished in a passionate torrent . . . like a bobolink on a reed";[2] or struggling out of a glacier field on a stormy Alaska day, accompanied by a courageous little dog, Stickeen.[3] Many of

Muir's writings are collected by Edwin Way Teale in *The Wilderness World of John Muir* [422]. See also Muir's *The Mountains of California* [286]; *Our National Parks* [283]; *My First Summer in the Sierra* [285]; *The Story of My Boyhood and Youth* [287]; and *Travels in Alaska* [288]. Linnie Marsh Wolfe's Pulitzer Prize-winning biography, *Son of the Wilderness* [470], has been joined by three recent books on Muir, who, in addition to his writing, founded the Sierra Club, popularized the preservationists' cause at Hetch Hetchy, and thus became one of the architects of the national park system. See Fox, *John Muir and His Legacy: The American Conservation Movement* [133]; Turner, *Rediscovering America: John Muir in His Time and Ours* [431]; Cohen, *The Pathless Way: John Muir and the American Wilderness* [29]. See also Jones [192] and Richardson [345].

Gifford Pinchot   Gifford Pinchot, a contemporary of Muir, approached resources policy from the direction of conservation, rather than Muir's preservation. Pinchot, Forest Service chief during the Theodore Roosevelt administration, believed in expert management of natural resources. The nation would achieve "the greatest good for the greatest number" through the use of government policy to harness rivers, regulate grazing on the public range, and control the supply of timber and minerals. This conceptualization meant that federal regulation should be an instrument to achieve a balanced policy of exploiting and conserving resources so that wise economic use could be made of them both for current and future generations. The object of Pinchot's policy was "the little man"—the homebuilder, the small farmer and rancher, and local businesses and residents. Thus conservation, in Pinchot's terms, might require that a forested area within a national forest remain uncut, but his justification—contrary to Muir's—was that the value of the wood products contained there would be maximized if used by future generations rather than by this one.

Pinchot is so preeminent in natural resources policy that it seems that nearly every interest group, at some point, claims to be the heir to the Pinchot legacy. As just suggested, however, Pinchot did not try to be all things to all people, and the time taken to understand Pinchot and the ways in which his approach differs from other resource philosophies is well spent. Sources on natural resource theory are presented in Chapter 5. The autobiography of this brilliant, tenacious, and entirely self-assured (or arrogant, take your choice) early leader is *Breaking New Ground* [326]. His activist personality is showcased in *The Fight for Conservation* [325], published in 1910, just after his much-publicized firing by President William Taft. This polemic, which argued for expanding the Forest Service's authority, was undoubtedly intended to influence major Supreme Court litigation pending at the time.[4] One of the major works in resource policy and history is Samuel P. Hays, *Conservation and the Gospel of Efficiency* [161], in which the author hones in on Pinchot's ardent faith in expertise and management and concludes that the nation receded from the Pinchot approach in the decades following the chief's stormy departure. Pinchot's career is also discussed at length in the standard sources on the Forest Service. See The Forest Service later in this chapter.

John Collier   Collier was appointed commissioner of Indian Affairs by President Franklin Roosevelt in 1933. He was like Pinchot in many respects—able, activist, charismatic, and strong-headed—and succeeded in obtaining congressional approval of a legislative package that changed the face of federal Indian policy. The centerpiece of the "Indian New Deal" was the Indian Reorganization Act of 1934, which brought the allotment policy to an end and promoted tribal self-government. Other federal initiatives bolstered the progress of Indian people in such areas as education, health, and economic development. Kenneth Philp [323] and Lawrence Kelly [203] have both written able accounts of Collier and his times. Collier's own writing is also useful. See, for example, *The Indians of the Americas* [81]; and "The Genesis and Philosophy of the Reorganization Act," in *Indian Affairs and the Indian Reorganization Act, The Twenty*

Year Record [82].

The Indian reorganization era, for all of its accomplishments, remains controversial. Collier's zeal led him to press tribes to adopt Anglo-style constitutions and government councils. On several reservations, this pressure drove traditional councils underground. Within some tribes, the resulting splits have yet to be healed. Some of these issues are raised in a recent popular work by Peter Matthiessen, *Indian Country* [260]. But it is also hard to deny that the Collier program—although interrupted by the termination era of the 1950s—laid the foundation for the resurgence of tribalism that began in about 1960. A useful retrospective, published in 1986, examines this rejuvenating era [324].

Political Figures of the 1960s, 1970s, and 1980s The last quarter-century has brought sweeping changes to policy in the American West. Congress has made reforms in many areas, such as Forest Service and Bureau of Land Management authority, mining, timber harvesting, grazing, water policy, wildlife protection, wilderness and recreation policy, Indian law, immigration policy, and Alaska lands distribution. It has also been a time of great activity at the state level.

Although several recent books offer evaluations of some congressional leaders (see note 4 in Chapter 2), the events are still recent enough that the definitive biographies have yet to be written on most of the principal figures: Wayne Aspinall of Colorado, Lee Metcalf of Montana, Henry Jackson of Washington, Mark Hatfield of Oregon, and Morris Udall of Arizona. One happy exception is Richard Baker's book on the career of Clinton P. Anderson [23], the independent, conservation-minded New Mexico senator who will surely be smiled upon by history. For Anderson's engaging autobiography, see *Outsider in the Senate: Senator Clinton Anderson's Memoirs* [18]. Among those who have held high federal administrative positions, perhaps the dominant figures are three interior secretaries: Stewart Udall, who held the office from 1961 through

1969, longer than anyone except Harold Ickes during the New Deal, and who authored *The Quiet Crisis* [433], an acclaimed call for stronger environmental policies; Cecil Andrus, who presided over the Alaska land distribution; and James Watt, who symbolized the Sagebrush Rebellion. Three multiterm, former western governors, Tom McCall of Oregon, Dick Lamm of Colorado, and Bruce Babbitt of Arizona, have been notably influential. McCall, who was the principal figure in the cleanup of the Willamette River, the adoption of Oregon's statewide land-use legislation, and the state's bottle bill, has written an engaging autobiography—*Tom McCall: Maverick* [261]. Lamm coauthored *The Angry West* [220]. Among other things, Babbitt has conceived of the notion of "public use," which he believes will replace "multiple use" as the basic resource philosophy on federal lands.[5] State administrative officials, such as New Mexico's state engineer, Steve Reynolds, have wielded great power in the resource arena. The work of these and other leaders during this dynamic era will undoubtedly prove to be fruitful ground for autobiographies, biographies, and other commentary in upcoming years.

Wallace Stegner Stegner's gigantic and diversified life's work is the mother lode of wisdom on the American West. His nonfiction includes the monumental analysis of water, climate, and political geography, *Beyond the Hundredth Meridian: John Wesley Powell and the Second Opening of the West* [396]; a compelling history of the Mormon Trail, *The Gathering of Zion* [398]; a biography of his mentor, Bernard DeVoto, *The Uneasy Chair* [401]; and a collection of shimmering essays on conservation, *The Sound of Mountain Water* [399]. Stegner also served as editor for *This is Dinosaur: Echo Park and Its Magic Rivers* [403], an evocative argument against the proposed Echo Park Dam; a copy of this work was placed on the desk of every representative and senator during the controversy of the mid-1950s, which, as well as any other, marked the birth of the modern environmental movement.

In spite of these works, Stegner is first and foremost a novelist, having collected the Pulitzer Prize and the National Book Award (but not yet the Nobel Prize—a fact that specialists in western literature offer as proof positive of outsiders' myopia toward the intellectual accomplishments of the American West). Slowly and steadily, page-by-page, without fanfare, his *The Big Rock Candy Mountain* [395], *Wolf Willow* [397] (described by Stegner, not as a novel, but as "a history, a story, and a memory"), and *The Spectator Bird* [402] accumulate frank, lucid observations on day-to-day life in the West—offering images painted with subtlety and indirection. *Angle of Repose* [400] is even more. This great novel, based on the late nineteenth-century letters of the remarkable Mary Hallock Foote, is a grand panorama of the West, an epic containing so much that most readers will be left with a head-shaking awe of the talent that produced it.

One logical way to go about reading Wallace Stegner is simply to go through his clean, direct prose—fiction and nonfiction—in chronological order. Then, both as review and as new insight, a person could read *Conversations With Wallace Stegner* [404], Richard Etulain's far-ranging taped interviews with Stegner. Also, the Winter 1985 issue of the *South Dakota Review* [391] is devoted entirely to Stegner, with essays on various aspects of his life and work. A person will then have the basic literary stock in trade for understanding the American West: a rendering of the flow of history; images both of the region's glory spots and of its staid, dignified plains; accounts of heroism and of the unglamorous daily lives of westerners; repeated calls for cooperation among divisive elements; and principled entreaties to fend off the zeal of the onrushing boosters, whose ventures would homogenize the region, thus stripping it of the common and uncommon qualities that Stegner conclusively proves to be in such abundance beyond the 100th meridian.

The Subcultures

American Indians   Many non-Indians are baffled by the fact that Indians press so hard to maintain the reservation system, where poverty seems to be omnipresent, educational services and housing inadequate, and alcoholism rampant. And, to be sure, in spite of the many gains by the tribes during modern times, such stereotypes continue to hold all too much truth. But there are many reasons, tangible and intangible, why Indian leaders see the reservations as the premise for the future progress of their people. Indians are "haves" in just one respect—land—and they consider development of tribal natural resources, including recreation, to be the most logical path toward rebuilding tribal economies. Indian leaders believe that tribal governments can best detect and meet the social needs of Indian people. Then too, reservation life has positive aspects to it—a web of family, special backcountry places, tradition, and mysticism—that Indian people are determined to preserve and improve. The reservations are homelands.

In the late 1960s, as Indian tribes were regrouping from the termination era's assault on the reservation system, Vine Deloria, Jr., wrote *Custer Died for Your Sins* [95], setting out the modern policy goals of Indian tribes. The book is a forceful, poignant, and often humorous call for tribal sovereignty in Indian country and for a substantial federal financial commitment to bolster reservation economies and to fulfill treaty promises. Remarkably, *Custer* is not dated nearly two decades after it was written. It remains a fine source for gaining a sense of the aspirations of Indian people.

The ambiguities, subtleties, and contradictions of reservation life are explored in objective, insightful fashion by young, award-winning Indian novelists Louise Erdrich, *The Beet Queen* [120], *Love Medicine* [119]; James Welch, *Winter in the Blood* [457]; Leslie Marmon Silko, *Ceremony* [378], *Storyteller* [379]; and N. Scott Momaday, *House Made of Dawn* [278]. D'Arcy McNickle, *They Came Here First* [267], and Frank Waters, *The Man Who Killed the Deer* [444], *Book of the Hopi* [446], have written piercingly on the deeply traditional pueblos of the Southwest. See also Borland, *When the Legends Die* [41]. A number of books offer valuable perspectives on contemporary life among Alaska Natives in rural Alaska. See, for example, Berger, *Village Journey: The Report of the Alaska Native Review Commission* [32]; Boeri, *People of the Ice Whale: Eskimos, White Men, and the Whale* [40]; Nelson, *Make Prayers to the Raven: A Koyukon View of the Northern Forest* [304].

Hispanics   Beginning as early as the sixteenth century, Hispanics moved north into what is now the United States through four main corridors: the California coast, the Santa Cruz River in southern Arizona, the Rio Grande River through New Mexico up into southern Colorado, and southeast Texas, along the coast of the Gulf of Mexico. Some of the missions and settlements have disappeared, some have expanded into major urban areas (Los Angeles, Tucson, Santa Fe, and San Antonio are examples), and others remain distinctly Hispanic communities (towns in northern New Mexico and southern Colorado's San Luis Valley are among the most notable). Movement of Hispanic people across the border remains a major domestic and international issue.

Hispanic issues in the Southwest are given broad treatment in two anthologies. See Weber [455]; Cafferty and McCready, *Hispanics in the United States: A New Social Agenda* [53]. On immigration, see McWilliams [273], and Kiser and Kiser [212]. Mexican poet and essayist Octavio Paz has examined Mexican culture in *The Labyrinth of Solitude: Life and Thought in Mexico* [320]. Recent studies have explored close-knit Hispanic *barrios* where the language, religious traditions, and culture remain intact. See Romo, *East Los Angeles: A History of a Barrio* [353]; and Camarillo, *Chicanos in a Changing Society* [56]. For a thorough bibliography, see Valk [487].

John Nichols provides a hard-hitting account of the destruction of Hispanic culture in the not-so-fictitious towns of Milagro and Chamisaville. The first and best of Nichols's three novels, which compose his New Mexico Trilogy, is *The Milagro Beanfield War* [306], a brilliant, often hilarious treatment of the relationship among Hispanic people, land, water law and policy, and the effects of drawing traditional subsistence peoples into the cash economy. The other novels in the trilogy are *The Magic Journey* [307] and *The Nirvana Blues* [308]. The rich traditions of the Hispanic Southwest have provided the fiber for several other outstanding works of fiction, among them Rudolfo Anaya's *Bless Me, Ultima* [16]. See also Anaya, *The Silence of the Llano* [17]; Harth and Baldwin, *Voices of Aztlan: Chicano Literature of Today* [158]; and Cather, *Death Comes for the Archbishop* [62]. George Sanchez's compelling piece, *Forgotten People* [360], argued for reforms, including a land-grant program, to remedy the bleak situation of rural Hispanic New Mexicans. The book has been called the cornerstone of the modern Chicano movement. *Forgotten People* is complemented by the more recent *Los Primeros Pobladores: Hispanic Americans of the Ute Frontier* [416] by Swadesh. See also Briggs and Van Ness, *Land, Water and Culture: New Perspectives on Hispanic Land Grants* [44].[6]

Mormons   The history and present of the West are fundamentally incomplete without an understanding of the Mormons and their Church of Jesus Christ of Latter-Day Saints. The overland migration of the Mormons from Nauvoo, Illinois, to Salt Lake City in 1846 and 1847 was one of the turning points in the region's history; Brigham Young was one of the most influential personalities; and the LDS Church is one of the West's most powerful institutions. Today, Mormons dominate the government and economy of Utah, exert major influence in Nevada, Idaho, and Arizona, and play key roles on selected political issues in several other western states.

In *The Year of Decision: 1846* [97], Bernard DeVoto recounts the expulsion of the Mormons from Illinois, an event he considers one of the key occurrences in the tumultuous times of the late 1840s. A fuller treatment of the Mormon Trail is Stegner's *The*

Gathering of Zion [398], which includes a thorough bibliography. See also Stegner's *Mormon Country* [394]. For a poem by Susan Snively about the thirteenth wife of Brigham Young, who carried the same name, see, "For the Thirteenth Wife (Susan Snively, 13th Wife of Brigham Young)" in *From This Distance* [387]. Two recent works deal with the contemporary influence of the Mormons. *The Mormon Corporate Empire* [165] by John Heinerman and Anson Shupe explores the vast Mormon political and financial network, but sees those workings only as a means to an end: "[T]he LDS Church's goals have not mellowed or narrowed, even late into this century. The Church is still engaged in a crusade to bring about a theocracy in the United States."[7] But this, like the other sources cited here, is not an anti-Mormon tract, for the authors plainly respect the Mormons' seemingly congenital industriousness, thrift, and friendliness. Gottlieb and Wiley [143] ably cover much of the same ground.

Asian-Americans People traveled from China to the Gold Country as early as 1848 and, when the gold played out, Chinese immigrants constituted much of the labor pool for the building of the transcontinental railroads. All the while, as miners, construction workers, farmers, or urban residents, they suffered the rawest forms of discrimination. The Japanese, who emigrated in the 1890s, were the next group to arrive in numbers from Asia; most of them became laborers and farmers in the first generation. They were subjected to internment during World War II. Immigrants from Asia have also included Filipinos, Koreans, and the modern "boat people."

The experiences of Asian-Americans in the mining camps, on the railroads, on the farms, in the canneries, and in the internment camps all directly raise distinctively western issues. More recently, a regional development of considerable importance has been the ability of Asian-Americans, most of whom have settled in urban areas on the Pacific Coast, to overcome racial hostility and cultural differences and to achieve success in the majority society. See, for example, Maxine H. Kingston's *The Woman Warrior: Memoirs of a Girlhood Among Ghosts* [209] and *China Men* [210]. The story of Asian-Americans in the western United States is given broad coverage in *Becoming Americans* by Tricia Knoll [218]. Jack Chen treats the Chinese experience in depth in *The Chinese of America* [64]. The leading work on the internment of the Japanese during the 1940s is Michi Weglyn's *Years of Infamy: The Untold Story of America's Concentration Camps* [456]. See also *Personal Justice Denied: Report of the Committee on Wartime Relocation and Internment of Civilians* [434]; and Tateishi's *And Justice for All: An Oral History of the Japanese American Internment Camps* [419]. The creation of a Chinese and, later, Mexican "peasantry" on the big farms in California is the subject of *Bitter Harvest* [89] by Cletus E. Daniel.

Farmers, Ranchers, and Cowboys The ranches and farms of the West have many and diverse impacts on the region. They contribute to overriding resource problems by causing the loss of topsoil and by polluting streams with silt and agricultural chemicals. Because they use 90 percent of all western water, farmers and ranchers created the demand for the large water projects that are at the center of so much controversy. Yet these industries are the foundation for local economies and provide food for the nation and the world. They preserve open space. As a culture, the people of the ranches and farms have settled in so deeply and for so long that for all practical purposes they are indigenous societies.

In his essay, "Cowboys, Indians and the Land of Promise" [38], western historian Ray Allen Billington examines the myth and reality of ranch life. Ivan Doig's exquisite *This House of Sky* [103] and *English Creek* [104], and *Dancing at the Rascal Fair* [105], are set in small ranching and farming communities in Montana. Gretel Ehrlich's *The Solace of Open Spaces* [113], which depicts modern ranch life, is nothing short of a masterpiece. If there is romanticism there, it is a romanticism bred of hard work, attention to detail, stark plains landscapes, and the steady tendering of personal relationships.

> Winter scarified me. Under each cheekbone I thought I could feel claw marks and scar tissue. What can seem like a hardshell veneer on the people here is really a necessary spirited resilience. One woman who ran a ranch by herself had trouble with a neighbor who let his cattle in on her pastures. She rode out one morning to confront him. When he laughed, she shot the hat off his head. He promptly gathered his steers and departed. "When you want that hat back, it'll be hanging over my mantel," she yelled as he loped away. When he suffered a stroke a few months later, she nursed him, though his hat still hangs over the fireplace today.
> Living well here has always been the art of making do in emotional as well as material ways. Traditionally, at least, ranch life has gone against materialism and has stood for the small achievements of the human conjoined with the animal, and the simpler pleasures—like listening to the radio at night or picking out constellations. The toughness I was learning was not a martyred doggedness, a dumb heroism, but the art of accommodation. I thought: to be tough is to be fragile; to be tender is to be truly fierce.[8]

There are hundreds of western communities dependent on resource-based economies other than farming and ranching—logging, mining, commercial fishing, and recreation. Jim Harrison's *Legends of the Fall* [157], Thomas McGuane's *Nobody's Angel* [264], and Norman MacLean's *A River Runs Through It* [252] are fine works of fiction set in such locales. *Sometimes a Great Notion* [208], Ken Kesey's epic novel, deals with the stresses in a western Oregon timber community.

The Institutions

The Forest Service The Forest Service has long been a peculiarly influential western institution because of the attention it received under its first director, Gifford Pinchot, and because of its many powers and responsibilities as the directing agency for the national forests, which are such a basic part of the West's economy and society. The literature is extensive. The sources on Pinchot have already been discussed earlier in this chapter. The standard, and nicely written history, by Harold Steen [393], is thorough, accurate, and perceptive. Glen Robinson has written a fine study of agency processes, *The Forest Service* [348], completed in 1975 but still highly useful. Other books on the Forest Service include LeMaster, *Decade of Change: The Remaking of Forest Service Statutory Authority During the 1970's* [227]; Barney, *The Last Stand: Ralph Nader's Study Group Report on the National Forests* [25]; and Dana and Fairfax, *Forest and Range Policy* [88]. My *Land and Resource Planning in the National Forests* [463], co-authored with H. Michael Anderson, is burdened with some reasonably extended and dreary legal discussions, but the book also contains a goodly amount of history of the Forest Service and the national forests. In *Reforming the Forest Service* [315], Randal O'Toole has incisively applied economic analysis to demonstrate how the statutory framework is a major cause of the Service's bias toward timber cutting. I find some of his reform proposals to be of dubious merit, but his assessment of the underlying problems is true to the mark.

There has always been something of a mystique surrounding the forest ranger. Kaufman's *The Forest Ranger* [200] is a classic, and three decades after publication it remains an insightful study of institutional behavior and of the place of forest rangers in western communities. Inevitably, the fiction of the region is sprinkled with references to rangers, one good example being Doig's *English Creek* [104], based on the life of a Montana forest ranger and his family.

The Navajo Nation   The Navajo Nation, which owns most of northeastern Arizona and reaches into Utah and New Mexico, is by far the largest Indian tribe. The reservation covers more than 16 million acres (an area larger than twelve states) and has a population of nearly 200,000 tribal members; over 25 percent of all American Indian land is Navajo land and more than 10 percent of all American Indians are Navajos. Although, like most tribes, the Navajo is plagued by widespread poverty and high unemployment, the tribe is prominent in the economy of the Southwest due to its large land base; extensive stores of oil, gas, coal, uranium; and substantial, although unquantified, reserved water rights. Indian tribes across the West are exercising their recently rediscovered powers of self-government, but the Navajo Nation probably has gone further than any other tribe in gaining political control within its boundaries.

Peter Iverson's recent book, *The Navajo Nation* [188], is a thorough and fair treatment of the modern Navajo Nation. Parman's *The Navajos and the New Deal* [317] is a solid historical account. Other books cover various aspects of this fascinating tribe, a lens through which one can view many of the obstacles and potentials at work in Indian country today. See, for example, Kelly, *The Navajo Indians and Federal Indian Policy, 1900–1935* [202]; Zolbrod, *Diné Bahanè: The Navajo Creation Story* [478]. The detective novels of Tony Hillerman, set in the Four Corners area and based on the exploits of Sergeant Jim Chee of the Navajo Tribal Police, are delightful. See, for example, *The Dark Wind* [171].

The Weyerhaeuser Company Fortunes were made during the nineteenth century by those who were able to obtain federal land and resources directly from the federal government. Some engaged in pure fraud; others, such as the railroads, drove hard bargains with Congresses that were profligate with public resources, at least by modern standards; still others, such as the ranch cattle industry, used a combination of lax federal laws and violence, or the threat of it, to build their empires. See, for example, "The Big Four" in Chapter 2. By the turn of the century, however, federal oversight began to tighten in reaction to corporate abuses and most of the companies that have since risen to positions of power have taken different paths than their predecessors.

The Weyerhaeuser Company, which exerts broad influence over western timber policy, is a leading example of the modern companies. *Timber and Men* [168], an overly sympathetic but thorough corporate history, explains how Frederick Weyerhaeuser came to the Pacific Northwest in the late nineteenth century after the railroad grants and various federal timber statutes had effectively created a glut on the market. This was exactly the time when the timber stands in the Great Lakes had been mostly logged over and the nation necessarily had begun to look west for its timber supply. In 1900, Weyerhaeuser was able to raise the capital to make one of the largest land purchases in American history—900,000 acres of timberland at $6 per acre from the Northern Pacific Railroad. The Weyerhaeuser Company was off and running, and today is admired both for its corporate efficiency and for its leadership in the research and implementation of high-yield forestry.

Of course, numerous other resource-oriented corporations are main players in the lobbying and economic development that pervade policymaking in the West. The combination of energy and construction companies that built the Alaska pipeline in the 1970s—a venture notably reminiscent of the heyday of the railroads—is the subject of *800 Miles to Valdez* [355]. As already noted, the omnipresent matter of water development, beginning with the construction of the Hoover Dam in the 1930s, was the arena for the rise of the "six companies" (including Bechtel, Kaiser, and Utah International) and the Bank of America, as treated in depth in Wiley and Gottlieb's *Empires in the Sun* [461].

The Sierra Club The modern environmental movement has been heavily influenced by the national organizations that have either been born since the late 1960s or have boomed in membership to such an extent that they have virtually remade themselves. The organizations composing the environmental movement's so-called Group of 10 are The Wilderness Society,

Sierra Club, National Audubon Society, National Wildlife Federation, Natural Resources Defense Council, Environmental Defense Fund, Environmental Policy Institute, National Parks and Conservation Association, Izaak Walton League of America, and Defenders of Wildlife. The Sierra Club exemplifies these organizations, which increasingly resemble substantial corporations in many respects and which wield great influence in the making of resource policy.

The history of the club, founded by John Muir and others in 1892, is detailed in *The History of the Sierra Club, 1892–1978* [80] by Michael Cohen and in *John Muir and the Sierra Club* [192] by Holway Jones. For an annotated anthology of articles on the Sierra Club, see Ann Gilliam, *Voices for the Earth: A Treasury of the Sierra Club Bulletin* [140]. Otherwise, there are few treatments of conservation organizations—the best of which are Stephen Fox's outstanding history of conservation and its philosophical premises, *John Muir and his Legacy: The American Conservation Movement* [133] and Samuel P. Hays's excellent treatment of the modern environmental movement, *Beauty, Health and Permanence: Environmental Politics in the United States, 1955–1985* [162]. See also Allin, *The Politics of Wilderness Preservation* [13]. One can be sure that the literature of environmental history will proliferate.

NOTES

1. See, for example, Hafen, *Broken Hand: The Life of Thomas Fitzpatrick, Mountain Man, Guide, and Indian Agent* [150]; Alter, *Jim Bridger* [14]; Gilbert, *Westering Man: The Life of Joseph Walker* [139]; and Favour, *Old Bill Williams: Mountain Man* [123], written by a Prescott, Arizona, lawyer. For biographies ot two of the most colorful mountain men, see Victor, *The River of the West: The Adventures of Joe Meek* [441] (biography of Joe Meek); Beckwourth, *The Life and Adventures of James T. Beckwourth* [30] (based on the original 1856 edition). The Arthur H. Clark Company has published a multivolume account of the fur trade, including biographical sketches of the partici-

pants. See Hafen, ed., *The Mountain Men and the Fur Trade of the Far West* (ten volumes) [153]. See also Hafen, *Mountain Men and Fur Traders of the Far West: Eighteen Biographical Sketches* [151], and Hafen, *Trappers of the Far West: Sixteen Biographical Sketches* [152]. For a general history, see also Chittenden, *The American Fur Trade of the Far West* (two volumes) [66]. Among the journals and diaries, Hasselstrom's *James Clyman, Journal of a Mountain Man* [159], *James Clyman, Frontiersman, 1792–1881* [74] edited by Charles L. Camp, and Osborne Russell's *Journal of a Trapper* [357] edited by Aubrey L. Haines, are of particular interest. See also Ruxton's *Life in the Far West* [358]. On the role of women in the fur trade, see Van Kirk, *Many Tender Ties: Women in Fur-Trade Society, 1670–1870* [440].

2. See Teale, *The Wilderness World of John Muir*, p. 186 [422].
3. Id. at pp. 277–296. See also Muir, *Stickeen: The Story of a Dog* [284].
4. See *Light v. United States* (1911) [237], finding that state fencing laws were inapplicable to national forests, and *United States v. Grimaud* (1911) [436], upholding Forest Service authority to issue administrative fines. Pinchot also had laid plans for test litigation to raise the issues finally decided in *Utah Power & Light Co. v. United States* (1917) [438], concluding that the doctrines of laches and estoppel were inapplicable against the United States.
5. See, for example, Coggins and Wilkinson, *Federal Public Land & Resources Law*, pp. 1055–1056 [77].
6. Blacks are another major ethnic group in the West and their contributions are many, from the early Spanish explorations to the fur trade to the modern times. Their impact has been greatest in urban centers such as Oakland, Los Angeles, and Denver, where Blacks have played instrumental roles in arenas as diverse as industrial development, organized labor, civil rights, education, health care, and the performing arts. The subject is discussed ably in W. Sherman Savage, *Blacks in the West* [365] and in William Katz, *The Black West* [199]. The case has not yet been made that there is a distinctively western Black identity or culture, but the issue is a fruitful one for continuing investigation.
7. See Heinerman and Shupe, *The Mormon Corporate Empire*, p. 4 [165].
8. Ehrlich, *The Solace of Open Spaces*, pp. 43–44 [113]. See also Ehrlich, *To Touch the Water* [112]; Steiner, *The Ranchers: A Book of Generations* [410]; Jordan, *Cowgirls: Women of the American West* [193]; Randolph, *Beef, Leather and Grass* [339]; Durham and Jones, *The Negro Cowboys* [111].

51

"Sierra Gate." Ranch country in the Sierra Valley in northern California. *Courtesy, Lynn Douglas, Johnsville, California.*

4

THE TERRAIN

The Natural Systems

The Major Watersheds   Political geography in the West—as determined by lines drawn to demarcate states, Indian reservations, or federal public land systems—seldom comports with the natural features that would make for the most workable governmental divisions. High mountain divides are eschewed as boundaries in favor of longitude meridians and latitude parallels. The Continental Divide is used as a state line just once, along a short stretch of the Idaho–Montana boundary. This failure to tailor sovereignty with geography assures, for example, continuing multijurisdictional combat over rivers. There are no remotely serious pending proposals to redesign state boundaries—it is far too late for that—but a person gains the truest sense of the West by understanding watershed, as well as political, configurations. Thus, we can expect a steady if slow increase in joint policymaking among governments within whole basins or sub-basins. In the West, because of the tilt of the land, the location of communities and transportation systems, and the way in which water implicates most development decisions, the watershed is the most logical unit for comprehensive, interrelated decisionmaking. The major river basins are the Upper Missouri, with the Yellowstone and Platte systems as the largest tributaries; the Arkansas; the Rio Grande; the Colorado, which touches Mexico and seven states from Wyoming to Arizona; the Sacramento–San Joaquin system in California; the Klamath of northern California and Oregon; and, by far the largest both in terms of flow and land area, the Columbia, with its main tributary, the Snake, which flows through Wyoming and Idaho before meeting the mainstem.

Perhaps the single most helpful book for looking at the whole culture, economy, and natural system of an entire watershed is Frank Waters's *The Colorado* [445], published in the Rivers of America series. Waters writes beautifully and, although the piece was published in 1946 and thus fails to include the megapolitics of modern water development, he captures the geography of the Colorado basin and its constituent subcultures, including the strong Indian presence. See also Watkins, *The Grand Colorado: The Story of a River and Its Canyons* [448]. A more scholarly work is Norris Hundley, Jr.'s valuable history, *Water and the West* [183]. In addition, see Weatherford and Brown, *New Courses for the Colorado River: Major Issues for the Next Century* [451]; and Fradkin [134]. Edwin Corle and others have written evocative pieces on the Colorado Plateau, including the mystical Four Corners area [84]. See also Zwinger, *Wind in the Rock* [479]; and Henderson, *Sun, Sand and Solitude* [167].

Paul Horgan's Pulitzer Prize-winning work on the Rio Grande, *Great River* [177], is both great literature and great history. On the Rio Grande basin, see also Nichols, *A Fragile Beauty: John Nichols' Milagro Country* [309]; Folk-Williams, *The Rio Grande* [129]; Mueller, *Restless River: International Law and the Behavior of the Rio Grande* [282]; Meyer, *Water in the Hispanic Southwest: A Social and Legal History, 1550–1850* [276]; DeBuys, *Enchantment and Exploitation* [94]; and Waters, *The Woman at Otowi Crossing* [447]. On the Columbia basin, another Rivers of America book, *The Columbia* by Stewart Holbrook [174], offers a well-written, comprehensive view. The sources on Pacific salmon (given later in this chapter) also deal with the Columbia River basin. There are few works that treat other watersheds and whole river systems but several pieces are useful. See, for example, Corle, *The Gila: River of the Southwest* [85]. Northern Lights Institute of Missoula, Montana, has produced a fine overview of the Upper Missouri basin. See Snow, *Boundaries Carved in Water: An Analysis of River and Water Management in the Upper Missouri Basin* [388].

The Great Plains   A plains environment—a relatively level and treeless area—extends from the foothills of the Rockies to the eastern hardwood region and also exists in the Southwest and the Great Basin. The term Great Plains traditionally has been used to describe the arid plains bordered on the west by the Rocky Mountain front and on the east by the 98th meridian. From north to south, this immense grassland extends well into both Canada and Mexico. The Great Plains has received special attention for several reasons: because of the formidable obstacles it presented both to settlers heading west and to those who wished to settle on the plains; because of the technological innovations it spawned in order to surmount the physical difficulties of the region; because of its relatively large historical and contemporary Indian populations; and because of its subtle beauty.

Walter Prescott Webb's *The Great Plains* [453] remains the standard source. In *The Wild Prairie: A Natural History of the Western Plains* [127], Tim Fitzharris documents the alteration of the natural plant and animal environment and notes that "today only a fraction of this life remains." Nevertheless, his exquisite photographs prove his other conclusion: "in many areas the big skies and rolling countryside still have the magic of unspoiled wilderness."[1]   The fiction is excellent, with Hamlin Garland [136][137], Willa Cather [60][61], O. E. Rölvaag [352], and Edna Ferber [124][125] being the best-known chroniclers of the region. Mari Sandoz [361][362], John Neihardt [302], and Louise Erdrich [119][120] have written powerful books on Indian societies of the

plains. Several other worthwhile pieces examine this remark-
able area, at once both outpost and heartland, wasteland and
big sky country. See, for example, Plowden, *Floor of the Sky: The
Great Plains* [328]; Sandoz, *Love Song to the Plains* [363]; Kraenzel,
The Great Plains in Transition [219]. There is also a periodical, *The
Great Plains Quarterly* [144], published by the University of
Nebraska–Lincoln since 1981.

The Great Basin   To the uninitiated, the Great Basin is likely
to be even harder to fathom than the Great Plains. This land-
scape, which has no outlet to the sea, is bordered on the east by
the Wasatch Range and other mountains of Utah; on the north
by the southern edge of the Snake River basin; on the west by
the Sierra Nevada; and on the south by a narrowing V, the
bottom of which is the Nevada segment of the Colorado River
watershed. As such, this dry, sandy region, where streams
dissipate in desert "sinks," includes half of Utah, southeastern
Oregon and southwestern Idaho, a long strip of California east
of the crest of the Sierra, and almost all of Nevada.

The Great Basin, and often its people, have tended to generate jeers, or at best, disinterest, by the majority society. The
Paiutes were called "digger" Indians by the whites who looked
contemptuously on their diet of roots and insects; the migrants
apparently never stopped to marvel at the palpable resource-
fulness of a people who could subsist under such conditions.
The Mormons were able to maintain their civilization at the
edge of the Great Salt Lake precisely because no one else wanted
it, and they continue to receive scarce recognition for their
undeniable success in settling such hostile country. Most
Americans, to the extent they think of the Great Basin at all,
view it as a worthless expanse of sagebrush and sand that must
be traversed at 70 miles per hour or more in order to reach Las
Vegas, Reno, or the Pacific Coast.

There is, of course, another side to the Great Basin. John
McPhee, in his magnificent *Basin and Range* [270], explains the
geography of eastern Nevada and, in the process, inculcates the

reader with the wonders of this scratchy country. Walter Van Tilburg Clark's novels, *The City of Trembling Leaves* [68] and *The Track of the Cat* [69], Robert Laxalt's *Sweet Promised Land* [225], and Rob Schultheis's *The Hidden West* [370], set partially in the Great Basin, are outstanding reading. Other sources explain the region in physical and historical terms. See, for example, Houghton, *A Trace of Desert Waters: The Great Basin Story* [179]; Cline, *Exploring the Great Basin* [73]; and Stegner, *Mormon Country* [394]. For a robust treatment of American deserts from an historian's perspective, see Limerick, *Desert Passages: Encounters with the American Deserts* [238]. One of the lesser known, but most arresting, continuing conflicts between Indians and whites has occurred at Pyramid Lake in Nevada. Since the early twentieth century, irrigators have diverted Truckee River water, the sole source of water for Pyramid Lake, out of the watershed. The diversion has threatened the 25-mile-long lake; the Pyramid Lake Band of Paiutes, whose reservation encompasses the lake; and the cui-ui and Lahontan cutthroat trout, two endangered fish species that depend on Truckee River water. The standard work on the situation at Pyramid Lake is Knack and Stewart, *As Long As the River Shall Run: An Ethnohistory of Pyramid Lake Indian Reservation* [216].

The Greater Yellowstone Ecosystem Yellowstone National Park, mainly in Wyoming but also reaching into Idaho and Montana, is one of many places where the neat lines on the maps fail to comport with the lay of the land or with actual land management needs. Proposed geothermal development outside park boundaries may threaten the famous geysers within the park. Various animals, including grizzly bears and large migrating elk and bison herds, move in and out of the park. Timber harvesting and oil and gas drilling are scheduled for the seven national forests that girdle the park. However, the larger issues of road systems, erosion, habitat disturbance, and noise are the same as if the proposed development were to occur within the park boundaries. The need for a broader view apparently traces to Frank Craighead, Jr.'s trailblazing research on grizzly bear habitat, *Track of the Grizzly* [86]. Increasingly, there is recognition that resource planning must take into account the whole 13 million acres of the Greater Yellowstone Ecosystem—the West's most dramatic headwaters country, embracing the Absaroka, Gallatin, Madison, Teton, and Wind River ranges and holding the sources of the Yellowstone, Gallatin, Madison, Snake, Green, and Wind rivers, and the Clarks Fork of the Yellowstone river. In his influential *Greater Yellowstone* [344], Rick Reese sets out the argument for ecosystem planning and management at Yellowstone.

In *The Yellowstone Story* [154], Aubrey Haines gives a good sense of the Yellowstone plateau. This comprehensive, two-volume chronicle is loaded with illustrations, maps, and charts, and has a complete bibliography. *Nature's Yellowstone* [27] by Richard Bartlett is a fine examination of the geological formation of the region over billions of years. *Mountain Time* [368] by naturalist Paul Schullery is a personal account of a love affair with this land. Schullery also is the editor of *Old Yellowstone Days* [369], a collection of readings on Yellowstone's early days. In *Wapiti Wilderness* [292], Margaret Murie offers memorable vignettes of her life in Jackson Hole, near the Grand Tetons. Alston Chase's *Playing God in Yellowstone* [63], a heated criticism of Park Service policy, was written recently enough that it is still too early to know whether the truth lies with the author's angry charges of mismanagement, the agency's loud denials, or somewhere in between.

The Pacific Coastline   "A coast," said T. H. Watkins in *On the Shore of the Sundown Sea* [449], "marks the boundary between what we know and what we can only guess, and is therefore a proper home for poets."[2] Watkins's book, itself often on the vague boundary between prose and poetry, brings out the magic of the California coast, both south and north. Many of Jack London's novels and short stories are set in the turn-of-the-century San Francisco Bay area, and give a sense of that vigorous society, tied in so many ways to the ocean and the bay. See, for example, London, *The Sea Wolf* [244]. See also Harold Gilliam, *Weather of the San Francisco Bay Region* [141]. One of the California Natural History Guides is a readable, profusely illustrated treatment of the animals of the northern California seashore. See Hedgpeth, *Introduction to Seashore Life of the San Francisco Bay Region and the Coast of Northern California* [164]. There are several sources on the coastal area of the Pacific Northwest. See, for example, McConnaughey and McConnaughey, *Pacific Coast* [262]. In *Children of the Raven* [160], H. R. Hays successfully presents the complex history and contemporary life of the Indian people of the Northwest Coast.

Alaska   Alaska, of course, is not a discrete natural system: it contains a great many separate natural systems (the state comprises nearly 18 percent of all land in the United States) and its eastern border with Canada is the 141st meridian, which arbitrarily cuts through major river drainages and mountain ranges. Nevertheless, Alaska raises a set of legal and policy issues that often are treated together, in spite of the conceptual and practical barriers to such an undertaking.

Alaska Geographic is the leading source for information on Alaska's many natural systems.[3] John McPhee's *Coming into the Country* [269] offers insight after insight into the land, people, and animals of Alaska; even old-time Alaskans concede that it is a remarkably accurate portrait of this great land. In *Going to Extremes* [263], Joe McGinniss attempts to create a book of roughly the same genre as *Coming into the Country*. McGinnis writes well and the book is lively but—true to its title—it presents somewhat more extreme (and less typical) portraits and is based on more limited personal experiences than is McPhee's book. Barry Lopez has received the American Book Award for *Arctic Dreams* [247], his lyrical account of the Arctic region. *Make Prayers to the Raven* [304] by Richard Nelson is an eloquent statement of nature and subsistence living from the point of view of the Koyukon people, Alaska Natives of the Yukon country of central Alaska. Two pieces by major figures in the early preservation movement, *Travels in Alaska* [288] by John Muir and *Alaska Wilderness* [255] by Bob Marshall, capture the spirit of Alaska's wild country, as does Jack London's novel, *Call of the Wild* [243]. See also Marshall's *Arctic Village* [253], and *Arctic Wilderness* [254], a collection of Bob Marshall's journals, manuscripts, and letters edited by his brother, George. In addition, London's *White Fang* [245] and *The Son of the Wolf* [242], set in the far north wilderness, are collections of tales about Alaska's tempestuous gold rush days. *Two in the Far North* [291] is an inspiring story of both Alaska and the romance of two leading conservationists, Margaret and Olaus Murie. Olaus Murie's writings on wildlife have become classics [293] [294] [295]. Another fine account is by Olaus's brother, Adolph Murie, *A Naturalist in Alaska* [290].

And, although one can understand why some academics dismiss Robert Service's poetry as doggerel, Service is simply too much fun to bypass. Just one example is the saga of Sam McGee, who sought solace from the winter cold "on a Christmas day [while] we were mushing our way over the Dawson trail":

> And there sat Sam, looking cool and calm, in the heart of the furnace roar;
> And he wore a smile you could see a mile, and he said: "Please close that door.
> It's fine in here, but I greatly fear you'll let in the cold and storm—
> Since I left Plumtree, down in Tennessee, it's the first time I've been warm."
> *There are strange things done in the midnight sun*
> *By the men who moil for gold;*
> *The Arctic trails have their secret tales*
> *That would make your blood run cold;*
> *The Northern Lights have seen queer sights,*
> *But the queerest they ever did see*
> *Was that night on the marge of Lake Lebarge*
> *I cremated Sam McGee.*[4]

The Commodity Resources

The American West is rich in natural resources and their economic development has always been a central part of the region's economy and society. The sources I discuss provide laypeople with an understanding of how the traditional commodity resources are put to use. Other resources, such as recreation, wilderness, wildlife, and the environmental values of water, are treated elsewhere.

Minerals At the beginning of the California Gold Rush, many of the immigrants were able to obtain the yellow metal without resorting to sophisticated equipment. Except for those instances in which the gold literally was visible to the naked eye, as it was to James Marshall in January 1848, early streamside miners separated the gold from the gravel with an assortment of relatively simple devices such as gold pans, sluices, and long toms. It was another matter, however, to remove placer deposits (loose minerals in soil) from mineral-bearing lands located away from the streams. Hydraulic hoses were trained on hillsides, which melted away under the powerful blasts of water. Quartz deposits (veins of precious metals embedded in rock) required deep shafts and pick-axe labor. Hardrock mining became mainly a corporate pursuit, a trend that accelerated with the use of open-pit mines to obtain copper and molybdenum.

Today, with most of the West picked over, the emphasis in hardrock mining is on high-technology processing methods, including the reworking of old tailings, sometimes a profitable enterprise as prices fluctuate. For the organic energy fuels (coal, oil, gas, tar sands, and oil shale), geologists use state-of-the-art methodology to identify land movements that trapped vast plant communities, such as swamp-forests and thick peat deposits, thereby sealing in great supplies of energy—the organic material then decomposed and was converted into fossil fuel. Thus, the energy industry places a premium on exploration through plate tectonics analysis, satellite imagery, and aerial photography, in addition to on-the-ground sampling and drilling.

Brian Skinner's *Earth Resources* [380], one volume in the Prentice-Hall series on the foundations of earth sciences, is a good basic work for learning about the locations and qualities of both metals and energy fuels. The standard introductory geology texts can also be helpful. See, for example, Press and Siever, *Earth* [331]; Dott and Batten, *Evolution of the Earth* [107]; Larson and Birkeland, *Putnam's Geology* [222]. The specialized material on plate tectonics is difficult reading. See, for example, Tarling, *Economic Geology and Geotectonics* [418]. The same is true for the advanced sources on the exploration and extraction of minerals, but they are solid resource books for explanations of how, for instance, an oil-drilling operation or an open-pit coal mine operates. See, for example, North, *Petroleum Geology* [312]; Peters, *Exploration Mining and Geology* [322]. On geothermal energy, which is likely to be of increased importance in the future, see Bierman, Stover, Nelson, and Lamont, *Geothermal Energy in the Western United States: Innovation vs. Monopoly* [37].

Water   Nearly all western development is water intensive. In most parts of the West, farms are built on irrigation water as much as on the land itself. Extensive supplies of water are essential for energy development, whether coal-fired (steam turns the turbines), nuclear (water is used for cooling), or hydroelectric (water power turns the turbines). In urban areas, water is necessary for municipal and industrial growth.

Rodman Paul explains the historical role of water during the Gold Rush days [318]. The physical facts about western water are set out in various government reports. See, for example, United States Water Resource Council, *Second National Water Assessment: The Nation's Water Resources, 1975–2000* [437]. *The California Water Atlas* [198] by William Kahrl is a monumentally well-conceived and thorough look at water and water resource development in California; one hopes that it will be replicated for other western states and watersheds. The techniques employed in irrigated agriculture are explained in depth in a technical piece by Withers and Vipond [469]. The matter of urban water use is treated comprehensively in a remarkable survey by John Folk-Williams, Susan Fry, and Lucy Hilgendorf, *Western Water Flows to the Cities* [128], which takes an in-depth, objective look at the current tensions over water in twenty western cities. The material on water conservation is burgeoning as demands increase. See, for example, California Department of Water Resources, *Water Conservation in California* [55]; Weatherford and Brown, *Water and Agriculture in the Western United States: Conservation, Reallocation and Markets* [452]; Engelbert, *Water Scarcity* [116]; and Shupe's "Waste in Western Water Law: A Blueprint For Change" [376]. See also *Western Water Made Simple* by High Country News [169].

Range   The science of range management is treated in several basic texts. See Vallentine, *Range Development and Improvements* [439]; Heady, *Rangeland Management* [163]; Stoddart, Smith, and Box, *Range Management* [412]. With a growing awareness of the consequences flowing from the large percentage of overgrazed rangelands in poor or fair condition, this seems to be a time of ferment and reassessment in public and private range policy. The impact of grazing on the water resource, including the pervasive problem of soil erosion, is treated in the well-illustrated *Rangeland Hydrology* by Branson, Gifford, Renard, and Hadley [43]. See also Wunder, *Working the Range: Essays on the History of Western Land Management and the Environment* [473].

Recently, there has been considerable attention given to the deterioration of riparian areas due to cattle grazing. See "Wetlands" in this chapter. The larger question of desertification in the United States, a substantial part of which is caused by poor grazing practices, is the subject of a booklet by David Sheridan, put out by the Council on Environmental Quality [375]. Two of the most spirited entrants in the policy debate over federal range policy are *Locking Up the Range* [236] by Gary Libecap, who argues for privatizing federal rangelands, and *Sacred Cows at the Public Trough* [126] by Denzel and Nancy Ferguson, who advocate much stricter controls on grazing by the ranching industry.

Timber   The timber resource varies dramatically throughout the West. In general, stands in the southern and central Rockies are of low marketability, although harvesting in easily accessible areas can be profitable because of lower road-building costs, a major capital expenditure for timber operators. The resource is considerably more valuable in some areas of northern Idaho, Montana, and the Alaska panhandle. But the commercial bonanza for western timber is in the Pacific Northwest. California's north coast holds major stands of cedar, spruce, and coast redwood—the tallest living thing in the world. In Washington and Oregon, the largest timber-producing states in the country, massive Douglas fir trees are a staple for the homebuilding industry. Half of all standing softwood timber in the nation is found in the national forests.

Marion Clawson, the highly respected economist with Resources for the Future, has written *Forests For Whom and For What?* [71], the quintessential primer on forest policy. Lucid, evenhanded, and comprehensive, this is the kind of short, foundational book that every technical field should be blessed with. The practice of silviculture (managing forests for the production of commercial wood products) is treated in a readable text, which explains all aspects of timber management from thinning to harvesting to slash removal to restocking. See David Smith, *The Practice of Silviculture* [383]. See also Daniel, Helms, and Baker, *Principles of Silviculture* [90]. Another text, *Forest Ecology* by Spurr and Barnes [392], deals with forests as ecosystems. For a discussion of old-growth stands, see the next section of this chapter. Several government reports provide statistics on the importance of private and public timber. See, for example, United States Forest Service, Department of Agriculture, *Forest Service, An Analysis of the Timber Situation in the*

United States, 1952–2030 [435]. A collection of essays on clear-cutting explains this controversial practice, environmentally destructive in some respects but necessary for the regeneration of some species, such as Douglas fir, which in most regions will not regenerate in their own shade. See Horwitz, *Clearcutting: A View From the Top* [178]. There are two extensive bibliographies on the timber resource. See Conservation Foundation, *Forest Land Use: An Annotated Bibliography of Policy, Economics, and Management Issues, 1970–1980* [83]; and Ogden, *The United States Forest Service: A Historical Bibliography, 1876–1972* [313].

The Animals and Plants

The commodity resources received attention first and, of course, they continue to be of great significance. Gradually, however, the public has come to acknowledge the worth of other kinds of resources. The following are examples of animals and plants, newly conceived of as "resources" also, that have come to the fore because of their value to hunters and fishers, other recreationists, and scientists; their beauty and spirituality; their intrinsic worth as discrete species or ecosystems; and, in many cases, their considerable economic importance.

The Grizzly Bear, the Wolf, the Bald Eagle, and the Pacific Salmon   These four animals have several common characteristics. Individuals roam widely and regularly across numerous jurisdictional lines, including international borders, making coordinated policymaking difficult. Until relatively recently, indiscriminate taking of grizzlies, wolves, eagles, and salmon was allowed, depleting their numbers or exterminating them altogether in some regions. All are sensitive to development, and their native ranges have been greatly reduced as their environments have been altered. These animals are magnificent and inspiring, and they make valuable contributions to the different natural systems within which they exist, but there are trade-offs for protecting them. Pacific salmon have substantial commercial value but so do their chief competitors for habitat, the dams that generate hydroelectric power. Grizzly bears, and perhaps wolves, can jeopardize human lives and both cause stock losses. Eagles prefer as habitat virgin old-growth forests, where the commercial value of timber is highest. The four epitomize the difficulties in reconciling powerful cross-currents in resource development, philosophy, and management.

The literature is extensive and much of it is of high quality. On grizzly bears, there are a number of fine books, all taking different approaches to the subject: *The Grizzly Bear: The Narrative of a Hunter-Naturalist* [472] by William Wright, which was published in 1909 but retains vitality as a balanced, readable, and at times humorous source; *Track of the Grizzly* [86] by Frank Craighead, Jr., a documentary account (for the general public) of scientific field studies in the Yellowstone ecosystem, which is highly critical of Park Service policies; *The Grizzly Bear* [266] by Thomas McNamee, which mixes scientific fact and fiction by tracing the activities of a hypothetical grizzly and her cubs from April, when they wake up from hibernation, to October, when they den for the winter; and David Brown's *The Grizzly in the Southwest* [47], a comprehensive treatment of the history of the grizzly in one region, but offering a fine foundation for the general subject of competition between grizzlies and human beings over habitat and options for resolving that competition. Bears, like politicians, seem to make excellent subjects for biographies. See, for example, Caras, *Monarch of Deadman Bay: The Life and Death of a Kodiak Bear* [57] (a biography of a particular bear—each chapter is a year in the bear's life); and Ernest Thompson Seton's, *The Biography of a Grizzly* [372] (The great naturalist's life story of Wahb, the grizzly, makes, I can attest, captivating out-loud reading for both a parent and six- and eight-year-olds.)

There are several readable scientific works on eagles and

their habitat. See, for example, Leslie Brown, *Eagles of the World* [51]; and Love, *The Return of the Sea Eagle* [248]. George Laycock's *Autumn of the Eagle* [226] discusses conservation of the species and searches out the more intangible qualities of these soaring, inspiring birds that symbolize our nation's ideals and draw out our ability to wonder.

Barry Lopez has made a major contribution to the literature on wolves with his compassionate, beautifully written *Of Wolves and Men* [246]. The standard text, done in a personal, anecdotal style, is L. David Mech's *The Wolf* [274]. See also Young and Goldman, *The Wolves of North America* [476]; Brown, *The Wolf in the Southwest: The Making of an Endangered Species* [48]; Adolph Murie, *The Wolves of Mount McKinley* [289]; and Clarkson, *Wolf Country: A Wilderness Pilgrimage* [70]. Perhaps the most widely read book on wolves is *Never Cry Wolf* [281], the stunningly humorous piece based on the experiences of Canadian biologist and author Farley Mowat.

The wild Pacific salmon is explored in epic terms in Bruce Brown's expansive *Mountain in the Clouds* [45]. It is powerful, thought-provoking reading. Several other books examine these extraordinary fish, whose life journey is thousands of miles long, in some cases all the way from the Idaho Rockies to the Gulf of Alaska and back. See Netboy, *The Columbia River Salmon and Steelhead Trout: Their Fight for Survival* [305]; and Courtland Smith, *Salmon Fishers of the Columbia* [382]. Also of note is the magnificently illustrated work by Childerhose and Trim, *Pacific Salmon and Steelhead Trout* [65].

Game and Nongame Species The fabulous animal populations of the American West were trumpeted to nineteenth-century easterners through the accounts of hunting expeditions such as those led by Prince Maximilian of Wied–Neuwied, Prussia, William Drummond Stewart, and Theodore Roosevelt. The exploits of Maximilian and Stewart are discussed in De-Voto [98] and in the sources in DeVoto's bibliography. Roosevelt's observations, set out in typically colorful style, are found in *Ranch Life and the Hunting-Trail* [354]. The concept that this wealth was in fact exhaustible took hold haltingly. Wildlife programs had been instituted in rudimentary form in most states by the late nineteenth century, but modern wildlife management was not born until the 1940s, when Aldo Leopold wrote *Game Management* [231]. In this landmark book, Leopold set out a comprehensive philosophy premised on the idea that good wildlife management depends on good habitat management.

The status of wildlife in the eleven western states and Alaska is examined in several books.[5] Wildlife management continues to focus in substantial part on recreational fishing, bird hunting, and especially, big game hunting. See generally Bean, *The Evolution of National Wildlife Law* [29]. For bibliographies on wildlife policy and management, see Coggins and Smith, "The Emerging Law of Wildlife: A Narrative Bibliography," in *Environmental Law* [75]; Coggins and Patti, "The Emerging Law of Wildlife II: A Narrative Bibliography of Federal Wildlife Law," in *Harvard Environmental Law Review* [76]; and Sigler, *Wildlife Law Enforcement* [377]. State "wildlife" agencies, in other words, traditionally have tended to be mainly hunting and fishing agencies. There are changes in the wind, however, fueled by powerful philosophical works by Aldo Leopold and others urging a broader look at wildlife.[6] State and federal agencies have begun to heed the admonition of Starker Leopold that "the rewards of a beautiful fall day afield are by no means the exclusive prerogative of hunters. As many or more people appreciate watching wildlife, with no intent of capturing or killing it."[7] As a result, professional wildlife management gradually has expanded to include endangered species laws and programs to improve the habitat of nongame species, endangered or not. See generally Bean [29].

Old-Growth Timber Stands As forest land has been cut over, attention has begun to focus not just on the amount of forest land per se but also on the dwindling amount of old-growth forest land: old growth is itself a discrete resource with different characteristics than second- or third-growth stands. Among other things, numerous animal species live only in old growth; the virgin stands possess extraordinary beauty; and the soils are spongier and contain more nutrients, because fallen trees blend into the earth rather than being harvested and renewed. These soil characteristics afford optimum watershed conditions for the steady run-off of clear and cool water, thereby producing major benefits for the economic and noneconomic uses of water. Maintaining old-growth stands, as opposed to replacing them with monocultures designed for commercial harvest, also promotes diversity of plant and animal species, which one leading source has described as "the heart and soul of conservation."[8] The Wilderness Society has published an excellent piece, with a bibliography, on biological diversity [460].

The depletion of the old-growth resource is the subject of Larry Harris's important book, *The Fragmented Forest* [156], in which the author analyzes current Forest Service policy in the Pacific Northwest, where most of the remaining commercial old-growth stands are found. He finds that the agency, by assuring the existence of only a limited number of isolated old-growth "islands," is threatening species diversity and the integrity of the old-growth resource. See also Maser [258]. In *The Klamath Knot* [442], David Raines Wallace has created a brightly etched portrait that extols the virtues of a diverse natural system, the Klamath Mountains, lying astride the western California-Oregon border.

Wetlands Wetlands are a distinctive group of habitats intermediate between aquatic and terrestrial ecosystems. These highly productive communities, which contain vegetation, animals, soils, and water, include marshes, swamps, estuaries, and riparian forests. The phrase riparian zone is commonly used to describe a key category of wetlands, the green ribbons of vegetation that accompany streams. Wetlands provide a wide range of benefits. They are crucial to the water resource for, as the visible upper terraces of complex hydrologic systems, they act as sponges and feed groundwater aquifers. The vegetation in riparian zones stabilizes stream bottoms and banks, thus preventing erosion; slows the flow of streams, thereby storing water and preventing floods; and helps filter the silt-laden run-off, thus assisting in the purification of water. In rangeland systems, riparian zones produce twenty or thirty times more forage than the uplands and are prime grazing lands for domestic stock. Wetlands are havens for wildlife, serving as essential habitat for migratory waterfowl and numerous other animals. In the American West, many of these fragile systems have been degraded by logging, grazing, water withdrawals, and land development. Whole wetland environments have been eliminated by landfills or water diversions.

The recent literature reflects the latter-day recognition of the wetlands resource and of its rapid degradation. Straightforward, objective pieces explain wetland ecology. See, for example, Niering, *Wetlands* [310]; and Etherington, *Wetland Ecology* [121]. Sources on groundwater and waterfowl explain the contributions of wetlands. See, for example, Wilson, *Groundwater: A Non-Technical Guide* [467]; Johnsgard, *Water Fowl of North America* [191]; and Brown, *Arizona Wetlands and Water Fowl* [46]. A real find is *Once a River* [340] by Amadeo Rea, which examines the ecology and cultural history of the Middle Gila River in Arizona, where water no longer runs. The book views just one stretch of river but it stands as a broad testament both to the wonders of riparian habitat and to the jeopardy in which western wetlands are placed by overdevelopment.

The Texture of the Ground

For most newcomers, the West, from the Sonoran Desert to bush Alaska, is something of an acquired taste. For them, most of the West is not Big Sky Country or the Great American

Desert: it is just plain desolate. This applies even to the grandeur of areas such as San Francisco Bay and the high Rockies. Transplants often find the dry, summer-brown hills of northern California less than they had expected from the land of milk and honey. The mountains of the West lack lush deciduous trees, and the glow of aspen groves during the fall may be perceived as a pale substitute for the colors of New England. It turns out there is a good deal more of such things as trailer homes, fast-food strips, and roadside trash than depicted in *Arizona Highways* or the coffee-table books.

Those who have written of the West during the past three decades have done an outstanding job of simply presenting the modern West—as is, without frills or pretensions. This aspect is the greatness of Edward Abbey's writing. The picaresque monkey wrenching, the high-speed chases, and the pro-environment tirades all raise, through hyperbole, justifiable questions about where the West is going—and they make exciting reading—but Abbey was first and foremost a person who loved the Southwest and wrote of it with great skill. There is utter honesty in the physical descriptions in *The Monkey Wrench Gang* [4], *Fire on the Mountain* [2], *Slickrock* (with Philip Hyde) [5], and *Desert Solitaire* [3]. These masterpieces are exultations of the beauty of high plains, desert, and rock canyons, of solitude, aridity, and space. In *The Brave Cowboy* [1], he managed to draw the reader into his book by his wordwork with a "burnt-out wasteland" consisting of a "rolling mesa of lava," a "rudimentary form of bunch grass," "the tough spiny yucca," and "a degenerate juniper tree . . . an under-privileged juniper tree, living not on water and soil but on memory and hope. And almost alone."[9]

Other contemporary writers have sketched out the texture of the ground in the many Wests. Several of the young writers are presented in an anthology, *Writers of the Purple Sage*.[10] The Montana literary tradition is showcased in the voluminous and splendid anthology, edited by William Kittredge and Annick Smith, *The Last Best Place* [215]. Kittredge's essays are collected in *Owning It All* [214] and *We Are Not in This Together* [213]. Norman MacLean's *A River Runs Through It* [252] is a justly acclaimed, unremitting delight. At various points in this work I have pointed to works by John McPhee, Wallace Stegner, Gretel Ehrlich, Rudolfo Anaya, David Raines Wallace, Louise Erdrich, Bruce Brown, Thomas McGuane, John Nichols, Gary Holthaus, Leslie Marmon Silko, William Kittredge, Ken Kesey, James Welch, and Ivan Doig. See also Pirsig, *Zen and the Art of Motorcycle Maintenance* [327]; Jack Kerouac, *On the Road* [205], *The Dharma Bums* [206]; Duncan, *The River Why* [110]; and leading poets such as Richard Hugo, *The Lady in Kicking Horse Reservoir* [181], *What Thou Lovest Well Remains American* [182], and Edward Dorn, *Slinger* [106]. Taken together, these and others have chronicled the land in a real and direct, yet enormously evocative, way. It is a wonderful body of literature.

NOTES

1. See Fitzharris, *The Wild Prarie: A Natural History of the Western Plains*, p. 7 [127].
2. See Watkins, *On the Shore of the Sundown Sea*, p. 113 [449].
3. See, for example, *Alaska Geographic*, volume 8, No. 3, "The Kotzebue Basin" [6]; *Alaska Geographic*, volume 10, No. 2, "Anchorage and the Cook Inlet Basin" [8]; *Alaska Geographic*, volume 10, No. 4, "Up the Koyukuk" [9]; *Alaska Geographic*, volume 11, No. 3, "The Chilkat River Valley" [10].
4. See Service, "The Cremation of Sam McGee," in *The Spell of the Yukon*, pp. 61–67 [371].
5. See, for example, Allen, *Our Wildlife Legacy* [12]; Nayman, *Atlas of Wildlife* [301]; Savage and Savage, *Wild Mammals of Northwest America* [364]; Adolph Murie, *A Naturalist in Alaska* [290]; Leopold, Gutierrez, and Bronson, *North American Game Birds and Mammals* [229].
6. See Aldo Leopold, *A Sand County Almanac* [232]; Trefethen, *An American Drusade for Wildlife* [425]; Amory, *Man Kind? Our Incredible War on Wildlife* [15]; Carson, *Men, Beasts, and Gods: A History*

of Cruelty and Kindness to Animals [58]; Matthiessen, *Wildlife in America* [259].

7. A. Starker Leopold and Tupper Ansel Blake, *Wild California: Vanishing Lands, Vanishing Wildlife*, p. 135 [230].
8. Id.
9. See Abbey, *The Brave Cowboy: An Old Tale in a New Time*, p. 1 [1].
10. See Martin and Barasch, eds., *Writers of the Purple Sage: An Anthology of Recent Western Writing* [256], which features several of the authors mentioned elsewhere in this book. The Introduction, id. at ix–xx, makes good reading in itself. It discusses trends in western literature and, among other things, thanks writers such as Wallace Stegner, Walter Van Tilburg Clark, Bernard DeVoto, A. B. Guthrie, Jr., Dorothy M. Johnson, Paul Horgan, and Frank Waters: They "had to confront the myths head on, to retell the Western stories in anti-mythological terms, to by God set the record straight." This freed up contemporary Western authors and allowed them to write about the West of today: "It was as if the contemporary region couldn't be addressed until the historical West had been correctly divined and defined in fiction." Id. at xi–xii (emphasis in original). For an exhaustive, nicely written reference work, see The Western Literature Association, *A Literary History of the American West* [458]. See also Etulain [480].

Members of the Traditional Kickapoo Band testifying in front of the Interior Committee of the House of Representatives. Jim Wahpepah of the Oklahoma Band of Kickapoos, lower right, translates from Kickapoo into English. Shortly thereafter, on January 8, 1983, President Reagan signed into law an Act recognizing the sovereign status of the Traditional Band and granting it a reservation. *Courtesy, Native American Rights Fund.*

THE IDEAS

The philosophical underpinnings of our society's approach toward the West have shifted over the century and three-quarters that federal policy has been at work. In this chapter I look at the ideas that have been, and are, major forces. Some have been in ascendancy during particular eras or in specific fields of policy. Some of them regularly war with each other, while others tend to be complementary. In some cases, it is possible to craft resolutions that reflect all of them in a more-or-less satisfactory fashion. With the caveat that different categories can fairly be drawn, it is well worth the while to sort out the basic policy imperatives that have shaped the American West.

Open Access to Public Natural Resources

Many of the policies of the nineteenth century were characterized by a laissez-faire approach that encouraged individual settlers and corporations, spurred by government subsidies, to obtain private vested rights in western land and resources. The premise—and it was proved correct if the goal was to promote the rapid settlement of the West by non-Indians—was that the public domain ought to be thrown open to private development, free of charge and unfettered by government regulation. These notions have proved influential and hardy. They remain deeply embedded in many areas of law and policy today, especially in regard to mining, water, and grazing. They also help determine federal timber policy and several aspects of wildlife policy. The perceived right—not infrequently viewed as divinely inspired—of the new immigrants to obtain western resources also was the driving force for the movements that led to allotment of Indian lands and to the breakup of Spanish and Mexican land grants.

Although numerous older books bugled the virtues of unrestricted and subsidized private development, it is now accepted by most that common pool resources (classic examples being rangelands, water, and wildlife) will be abused and depleted if free and unrestrained public access to them is allowed. This is the message of Garrett Hardin's famous article, "The Tragedy of the Commons" [155]. Nearly all of the authors who contributed to the spate of works about western resources in the past decade examine nineteenth-century laissez-faire policy and almost all of them explicitly reject it. See the sources noted at the introduction to Chapter 2. An example of how these ideas caused a specific law to be germinated, and then to become outmoded (although still in force), is John Leshy's excellent study of the General Mining Law of 1872 [233]. See also Kelley, *Gold vs. Grain: The Hydraulic Mining Controversy in California's Sacramento Valley* [201]. On a personal level, William Kittredge explores his own family's attempts to control nature in eastern Oregon in his fine collection of essays, *Owning It All* [214]. Advocates of private-sector development, of course, continue to press for unfettered commodity use of public resources, but legal and policy initiatives must now be pursued in a considerably different policy framework that includes a role for government regulation, market approaches prohibiting or restricting subsidies, and the other ideas that follow.

76

Resource Planning and Management

In the late nineteenth century, Gifford Pinchot and others began to make inroads on the extreme laissez-faire policies. Believing that expert planners and managers should direct the development of public resources, leaders of the conservation movement advocated and established governmental regulatory programs over timber, grazing, water power, and energy fuels. On Forest Service programs establishing regulatory control over timber and grazing during the early twentieth century, and on the adoption of legislation such as the Federal Power Act of 1920 and the Mineral Leasing Act of 1920, see generally Hays [161], Pinchot [325][326], Dana and Fairfax [88], and Coggins and Wilkinson [77]. Congress enacted sweeping planning and management legislation for the public lands in the 1970s and has installed the idea of a substantial degree of direction through federal planning as a major component of current federal policy.

The wisdom of planning and management by federal officials is, and surely will remain, a sharply disputed matter. In their writings, Pinchot [325][326], Aldo Leopold [231], and others argue that government direction is needed to prevent exploitation and to assure orderly resource development in generations to come. A growing number of resource economists, on the other hand, believe that federal involvement leads mainly to bureaucratic inefficiencies. See, for example, Stroup and Baden, *Natural Resources: Bureaucratic Myths and Environmental Management* [414]. One of the leading books in resource policy and history, Samuel P. Hays's *Conservation and the Gospel of Efficiency* [161], puts these issues in historical context, detailing the rise of conservationist philosophy during the Pinchot era and showing its strengths and limitations. Hays's book is perhaps the best starting point for analyzing the pros and cons of government regulation as opposed to a free-market regime. In the past few years the advocates of a provocative, if still theoretical and unproven, school of thought have proposed an approach that attempts to blend decentralization, environmental protection, and economic growth. The bioregionalism movement argues for local planning according to the carrying capacity of a watershed or other natural configuration in order to achieve sustainable societies based on gentle use. Bioregionalism is discussed, and a comprehensive bibliography offered, in Sale, *Dwellers in the Land: The Bioregional Vision* [359]. See also Gary Snyder's "Good, Wild, Sacred" [390] and *Turtle Island* [389].

Land and Species Preservation

Since the establishment of Yellowstone National Park in 1872, the United States has embarked on perhaps the most ambitious governmental preservation program ever undertaken. Among many other things, Congress has enacted sweeping endangered species legislation and has declared 88 million acres, about 4 percent of all land in the nation, as statutorily protected wilderness.

Preservation policy has spawned some of the best writing bearing on the American West. The definitive work on the wilderness idea and its development is Roderick Nash's *Wilderness and the American Mind* [299]. For a valuable compendium of facts on wilderness and wilderness management, see Hendee, Stankey, and Lucas, *Wilderness Management* [166]. One of the most intellectually exacting and forceful pieces in all of natural resource philosophy is *Mountains Without Handrails* [366], where Joseph Sax argues for wilderness preservation based on homocentrism—the notion that, whatever the benefits of wilderness for animals or the land itself, a strong preservation policy has profound benefits for human beings. Aldo Leopold, in his classic and compelling *Sand County Almanac* [232], places his stock in biocentrism, urging readers to "think like a mountain" and arguing for a "land ethic": "Examine each question in terms of what is ethically and esthetically right, as well as what is economically expedient. A thing is right when it tends to preserve the integrity, stability, and beauty of the biotic community. It is wrong when it tends otherwise."[1] See also Dasmann, *Environmental Conservation* [91], Rolston, *Environmental Ethics* [351], and the many articles in the journal, *Environmental Ethics* [118].

In *Progress and Privilege* [428], William Tucker makes a straight-on attack on the modern environmental movement. Tucker agrees that the environmentalists have accomplished needed reforms and have raised the public's consciousness, since about 1970. In this sharply written piece, however, he argues that environmentalists are essentially aristocratic and that their conservative, "flighty and nervous" approach has stalled technological progress. It is time, Tucker believes, for the country to move beyond environmentalism: "America can once again become the engine of the world's progress, its brightest and best hope for a better future."[2]

Market-Based Economics

There has been a sharp rise in interest in applying economic analysis to western resources issues, especially relating to public lands and water. Classic economic theory has been employed by diverse interest groups to numerous aspects of current policy. Some believe that government management of public resources and regulation of private development lead to massive inefficiencies. Others object to the longstanding subsidies to water, timber, range, and mining interests, arguing both that the subsidies are wrong on a distributive basis and that they contribute to the federal deficit. Such subsidies also are criticized on the ground that they lead to poor conservation practices because the artificially low cost for the use of natural resources gives no incentive to conserve the resources. Others attack subsidies in recreation, preservation, and wildlife policy and believe that such programs ought to be justified in market terms. Still others focus on externalities, such as the costs imposed on society by the pollution and erosion from industrial, mining, irrigation, and ranching operations, and look to the market as a mechanism for imposing environmental charges.

The literature on natural resources economics is expanding apace. Three schools deserve special mention. Resources for the Future (based in Washington, D.C.), with leading economists such as Marion Clawson, John Krutilla, and Allen Kneese, has produced a large corpus of highly respected work. See, for example, Clawson [71]; Kneese and Brown, *The Southwest Under Stress: Natural Resource Development Issues in a Regional Setting* [217]; and Martin, Ingram, Laney, and Griffin, *Saving Water in a Desert City* [257]. The Environmental Defense Fund has taken the lead among the environmental groups in applying market analyses to natural resources policy, especially in the area of western water. See, for example, Environmental Defense Fund, *Trading Conservation Investments for Water* [117]. Another leading example of the use of economics by environmentalists is Randal O'Toole's *Reforming the Forest Service* [315]. On the conservative side, writers calling themselves "the new resource economists" have produced several provocative pieces arguing, among other things, that the privatization of public lands would serve environmental as well as commodity needs. See, for example, Stroup and Baden [414]. One thing is sure: economic theory will continue to be a major factor in law and policy in the American West and, if anything, promises to grow in influence. See also Lecomber, *The Economics of Natural Resources* [228].

Ethnic Pluralism

There have been separatist movements throughout western history by groups such as the Mormons, the Hispanics who settled in the Southwest, and the Métis—the French-Indian mixed-bloods along the middle Canadian–U.S. border. On the

Métis, see, for example, Berger, *Fragile Freedoms: Human Rights and Dissent in Canada* [31]. Issues of ethnic pluralism continue in several contexts today. Hispanics, for example, press for bilingual education in the public schools and, especially in the Upper Rio Grande Valley, continue to cling to a considerable degree of local political autonomy exercised, among other things, through the *acequia*, the traditional communal mechanism for distributing water.[3]

American Indians, however, remain the minority group with the strongest legal, historical, and political claim to a substantial degree of governmental independence. Much of federal Indian policy can best be understood in terms of the tension between separatism and assimilation. In aboriginal times, tribes governed themselves, establishing societal norms, adjudicating wrongs, and punishing offenders. Three leading works on this blend of history, anthropology, and jurisprudence are Llewellyn and Hoebel's *The Cheyenne Way* [241], Reid's *A Law of Blood* [341], and Strickland's *Fire and the Spirits* [413].

Separatism was dominant during the establishment of the reservation system throughout most of the nineteenth century and during the "Indian New Deal" of the 1930s and 1940s, while assimilation was in the ascendency during the allotment era beginning in the late nineteenth century and during the termination era of the 1950s and 1960s. On the history of federal Indian policy, see generally Prucha [332][335][336][337], Washburn [443], and Dippie [102]. Beginning in the early 1960s, the tribes have made a vigorous push for self-determination in order to achieve control over natural resources, economic development, schools, adoptions, law and order, and religious practices within Indian country. The principle of Indian tribal sovereignty, recognized by the Supreme Court from the days of Chief Justice John Marshall through the 1980s, is explored in three recent books: Deloria and Lytle's *The Nations Within* [96], Barsh and Henderson's *The Road* [26], and my *American Indians, Time, and the Law* [462]. Fay Cohen, in *Treaties on Trial* [78], provides a comprehensive, insightful treatment of the modern

Indian fishing rights controversy in the Pacific Northwest. An older piece, more supportive of assimilationist philosophy, is Taylor's *The States and Their Indian Citizens* [421]. The tribes' recent success in establishing a considerable degree of self-government will be tested in future years, and an important element of the traditions and character of the American West will turn on whether Indian people are able to maintain the venerable institution of tribal sovereignty.

Cooperation

One of the myths is that the American West was settled by men setting out on their own: a lasting image is of a solitary man heading over a ridge, onward toward the Pacific. In fact, the early vanguards of Anglo-American migrants—the mountain men and the forty-niners—may have fit the stereotype, but permanent settlement was accomplished by families, working cooperatively in countless, steady, daily tasks to remake the frontier.

The scholarship on the place of women in the West has matured in recent years. The most extensive treatment is *Westering Women and the Frontier Experience* [296], in which Sandra Myres describes the experiences of Anglo, Hispanic, Black, French, and Indian women. Myres rejects polar stereotypical portrayals, both of the oppressed frontier woman and of the "sturdy helpmate," the heroine who "could fight Indians, kill the bear in the barn, make two pots of lye soap, and do a week's wash before dinnertime and still have the cabin neat, the children clean, and a good meal on the table when her husband came in from the fields—all without a word of complaint or even a hint of an ache or a pain."[4] Myres finds that both images are too broad-brush, born of revisionist history.

Other leading books in this diverse and essentially new body of writing include Susan Armitage and Elizabeth Jamison's effective attempt to create a multicultural perspective by beginning, not with the nineteenth-century arrival of Anglo woman, but with anthropological accounts of Indian and Hispanic settlements [19]; Lillian Schlissel's synthesis of more than ninety diaries to present a portrait of women's experience on the Overland Trail [367]; Julie Roy Jeffrey's analysis of the degree to which the personal and social benefits of the frontier flowed to women as well as men [190]; and John M. Faragher's conclusion, from a Marxist orientation, that western women were the losers in a class, race, and sexual struggle [122]. Two firsthand, nineteenth-century accounts by women have become classics— the *Shirley Letters* [67] and the reminiscences of Mary Hallock Foote [130]. Foote's unpublished letters were the basis of Stegner's *Angle of Repose* [400]. See also Luchetti and Olwell, *Women of the West* [249], which includes a memorable array of photographs. In all, this vigorous field of literature shows that there was a broad range of individual dreams and fears, accomplishments and failures, by a group of people who made largely anonymous but indispensable contributions to the gigantic task of settling a broad and hostile land.

The old stereotypes have been dimmed in another way. To be sure, the West has had far more than its share of violence, whether at Wounded Knee, Mussel Slough, Johnson County, or countless hundreds of other locales. But people worked together, too, and the country could not possibly have been settled otherwise. Today, many western towns are torn internally by new kinds of disputes, such as whether to develop or preserve natural resources. The subcultures of the West are at combat, with, for example, ranchers and farmers disputing the rights of Indians and rural Hispanics to possess and manage water rights outside of state law. In response, western writers, looking to the commonality engendered by a sense of place, have urged greater cooperation within local communities. Examples include Yi-Fu Tuan's *Space and Place* [427], Dan Kemmis's *Community on the Frontier* [204], Terry Tempest Williams's *Pieces of White Shell* [466], and my *The Eagle Bird: Searching for an Ethic of Place* [465]. In perhaps the single most profound passage on the American West, Wallace Stegner argues that westerners should look to the truest values of the past and apply them to the challenges of a new age.

> Angry as one may be at what heedless men have done and still do to a noble habitat, it is hard to be pessimistic about the West. This is the native home of hope. When it fully learns that cooperation, not rugged individualism, is the pattern that most characterizes and preserves it, then it will have achieved itself and outlived its origins. Then it has a chance to create a society to match its scenery.[5]

Geologic Time

Resource decisions have traditionally been made in terms of present needs. A Los Angeles or a Denver is considered expansive by assessing its water needs a generation hence. The 50-year projections in the forest plans now being developed by the Forest Service are praised for taking the long view but are essentially unreal to us because they push so far out: they try too much.

Not so for the geologist, who is trained to think in geologic time, to spread things out over tens and hundreds of millions of years. For a readable academic treatment of geologic time, see Eicher, *Geologic Time* [114]. In *Basin and Range* [270], John McPhee has made the concept of geologic time accessible to lay people. In this brilliant, broad-gauged book, one of the leading contributors to the literature of the American West explains plate tectonic theory through the device of travels through, and discussions with geology professor Kenneth Deffeyes about, the basin and range country of Nevada and western Utah. The lyrically written *Basin and Range* is a tour de force in every respect, opening the minds of McPhee's readers, forcing them back into deep time, showing how long it took these unprepossessing mountains and flatlands to evolve. Nearly all of his readers will come away imbued with a longer view, a sense that resource decisions are not quite as easy as they once seemed.

The most recent book from the prolific McPhee, *Rising from the Plains* [271], also works with concepts of time. He uses conversations with David Love, a geologist for the U.S. Geological Survey in Laramie, to recreate Love's life in south-central Wyoming and to build an understanding of the geology of the region. A third fine piece explicating geologic time is David Raines Wallace's *The Klamath Knot* [442], which explores the complex, diverse geology and terrain of the Klamath Mountains of northern California and southern Oregon.

This body of work, which articulates the single tick of homo sapiens' presence in the great reach of existence, is more intellectually unsettling, more humbling, more subtly but devastatingly critical of the extent of human arrogance than any written words I know. Yet geologic time, while it reduces our species, also unshackles us.

> A million years is a short time—the shortest worth messing with for most problems. You begin tuning your mind to a time scale that is the planet's time scale. For me, it is almost unconsious now and is a kind of companionship with the earth....
>
> If you free yourself from the conventional reaction to a quantity like a million years, you free yourself a bit from the boundaries of human time. And then in a way you do not live at all, but in another way you live forever.[6]

NOTES

1. See Leopold, *A Sand County Almanac, with Other Essays on Conservation from Round River*, pp. 224–225 [232].
2. See Tucker, *Progress and Privilege: America in the Age of Environmentalism*, p. 284 [428].
3. Acequias are discussed at various places in Meyer, *Water in the Hispanic Southwest: A Social and Legal History, 1550–1850* [276], and Brown and Ingram, *Water and Poverty in the Southwest* [49]. See also

Hutchins, "The Community Acequia: Its Origin and Development," [184].

4. See Myres, *Westering Women and the Frontier Experience*, 1800–1915, p. 3 [296].
5. See Stegner, *The Sound of Mountain Water*, p. 313 [399].
6. McPhee, *Basin and Range*, p. 129 [270].

Snow geese at Bosque del Apache National Wildlife Refuge, New Mexico.
By Bob Miles. *Courtesy, Arizona Game and Fish Department.*

6

Postscript: A Word on the Future of the West

The modern American West is a mosaic of all of these things, and many more. Some of them have formed and shaped public policy, and others will do so in the future. The texture of future laws will not come from the law itself but from these outside forces that, over time, will meld into the public consciousness and finally into law.

Over my short professional career—twenty-some years—I have become increasingly fascinated by the ways in which time works in the distinctive sphere of public policy affecting the American West. Certain principles became embedded in the law in the mid-nineteenth century and those laissez-faire notions survive yet, surprisingly intact. How powerful must be the forces that have kept those laws in place over so much societal change. Indian people lived in this region at least 12,000 years ago. Their sovereignty, too, remains partially intact in spite of all the wars waged against it by armies, churches, corporations, and legislatures. How powerful must be the passion of native people that has kept the idea of sovereignty alive.

But for me, the single most forceful concept is geologic time, as explained by John McPhee. Granted, we cannot make policy solely by geologic time. There are hundreds, thousands of other factors. But geologic time helps set the context. It tells us how long it has taken to construct what we have and how long we need to prepare for. It harnesses arrogance, breeds a fit conservatism.

McPhee, Stegner, and dozens of other modern writers of both fiction and nonfiction have made a contribution not yet widely recognized. They have assisted in defining a geographical region, in giving the West a sense of place, a sense of itself. When a people gains a sense of itself, wise decisions are likely to follow. Such improvements come in small increments, bit by bit, and it is still an open question whether policy in the American West will evolve quickly enough to outstrip the sheer and daunting numbers of people.

But at least the words and ideas are now there—and more good ones are sure to follow—so that westerners have access to a great amount of information about themselves, their surroundings, their common history, and their possibilities. It is an understanding of exactly those things that is the stuff of the best societies.

Bibliography

ITEM	AUTHOR & TITLE	PAGE NO.
1	Abbey, Edward. *The Brave Cowboy; An Old Tale in a New Time* (Albuquerque: University of New Mexico Press, 1977; orig. pub., 1956).	71, 73
2	Abbey, Edward. *Fire on the Mountain* (New York: Dial Press, 1962).	71
3	Abbey, Edward. *Desert Solitaire: A Season in the Wilderness* (New York: Ballantine Books, 1968).	71
4	Abbey, Edward. *The Monkey Wrench Gang* (Philadelphia: Lippincott, 1975).	9, 71
5	Abbey, Edward, and Philip Hyde. *Slickrock: The Canyon Country of Southeast Utah* (San Francisco: Sierra Club, 1971).	71
6	*Alaska Geographic*, volume 8, No. 3, "The Kotzebue Basin" (1981).	59, 72
7	*Alaska Geographic*, volume 8, No. 4, "Alaska National Interest Lands" (1981).	29, 59
8	*Alaska Geographic*, volume 10, No. 2, "Anchorage and the Cook Inlet Basin" (1983).	59, 72
9	*Alaska Geographic*, volume 10, No. 4, "Up the Koyukuk" (1983).	59, 72
10	*Alaska Geographic*, volume 11, No. 3, "The Chilkat River Valley" (1984).	59, 72

ITEM	AUTHOR & TITLE	PAGE NO.
11	Albright, Horace M. *The Birth of the National Park Service: The Founding Years, 1913–1933* (Salt Lake City: Howe Bros., 1985).	30
12	Allen, Durward Leon. *Our Wildlife Legacy* (New York: Funk & Wagnalls, rev. ed. 1962).	72
13	Allin, Craig. *The Politics of Wilderness Preservation* (Westport, Conn.: Greenwood Press, 1982).	50
14	Alter, J. Cecil. *Jim Bridger* (Norman: University of Oklahoma Press, rev. ed. 1962).	50
15	Amory, Cleveland. *Man Kind? Our Incredible War on Wildlife* (New York: Harper & Row, 1974).	72
16	Anaya, Rudolfo. *Bless Me, Ultima* (Berkeley, Calif.: Quinto Sol Publications, 1972).	43
17	Anaya, Rudolfo. *The Silence of the Llano* (Berkeley, Calif.: Tonatiuh-Quinto Sol International, 1982).	43
18	Anderson, Clinton P. *Outsider in the Senate:: Senator Clinton Anderson's Memoirs* (New York: World Pub. Co., 1970).	38
19	Armitage, Susan H., and Elizabeth Jamison, eds. *The Women's West* (Norman: University of Oklahoma Press, 1987).	82, 83
20	Arnold, Robert D. *Alaska Native Land Claims* (Anchorage: The Alaska Native Foundation, rev. ed. 1978).	28

ITEM	AUTHOR & TITLE	PAGE NO.
21	Athearn, Robert G. *The Mythic West in Twentieth-Century America* (Lawrence: University Press of Kansas, 1986).	3, 4, 9, 10, 22
22	Bakeless, John Edwin. *Lewis & Clark, Partners in Discovery* (New York: W. Morrow, 1947).	33
23	Baker, Richard A. *Conservation Politics: The Senate Career of Clinton P. Anderson* (Albuquerque: University of New Mexico Press, 1985).	38
24	Bakken, Gordon Morris. *The Development of Law on the Rocky Mountain Frontier: Civil Law and Society, 1850–1912* (Westport, Conn.: Greenwood Press, 1983).	10
25	Barney, Daniel R. *The Last Stand: Ralph Nader's Study Group Report on the National Forests* (New York: Grossman Publishers, 1974).	47
26	Barsh, Russel Lawrence, and James Youngblood Henderson. *The Road: Indian Tribes and Political Liberty* (Berkeley: University of California Press, 1980).	81
27	Bartlett, Richard A. *Nature's Yellowstone* (Albuquerque: University of New Mexico Press, 1974).	58
28	Bauer, K. Jack. *The Mexican War, 1846–1848* (New York: Macmillan, 1974).	23
29	Bean, Michael J. *The Evolution of National Wildlife Law* (Westport, Conn.: Praeger, rev. and expanded ed. 1983).	36, 68

ITEM	AUTHOR & TITLE	PAGE NO.
30	Beckwourth, James Pierson. *The Life and Adventures of James P. Beckwourth as Told to Thomas D. Bonner* (Lincoln: University of Nebraska Press, 1972; orig. pub., 1856).	50
31	Berger, Thomas R. *Fragile Freedoms: Human Rights and Dissent in Canada* (Toronto: Clarke, Irwin, rev. ed. 1982).	81
32	Berger, Thomas R. *Village Journey: The Report of the Alaska Native Review Commission* (New York: Hill and Wang, 1985).	29, 42
33	Berry, Don. *Trask* (New York: Viking Press, 1960).	34
34	Berry, Don. *A Majority of Scoundrels: An Informal History of the Rocky Mountain Fur Company* (New York: Harper, 1961).	34
35	Berry, Don. *Moontrap* (New York: Viking Press, 1962).	34
36	Berry, Mary. *The Alaska Pipeline: The Politics of Oil and Native Land Claims* (Bloomington: Indiana University Press, 1975).	28
37	Bierman, Sheldon L., D. Stover, P. Nelson, and W. Lamont, *Geothermal Energy in the Western United States: Innovation vs. Monopoly* (Westport, Conn.: Praeger, 1978).	62
38	Billington, Ray Allen. "Cowboys, Indians, and the Land of Promise" in *America's Frontier Culture: Three Essays* (College Station: Texas A & M University Press, 1977).	45

BIBLIOGRAPHY

ITEM	AUTHOR & TITLE	PAGE NO.
39	Billington, Ray Allen, and Martin Ridge. *Westward Expansion: A History of the American Frontier* (New York: Macmillan, 5th ed. 1982).	13
40	Boeri, David. *People of the Ice Whale: Eskimos White Men, and the Whale* (New York: Dutton, 1983).	42
41	Borland, Hal. *When the Legends Die* (Philadelphia: Lippincott, 1963).	42
42	Brack, Gene M. *Mexico Views Manifest Destiny, 1821–1846: An Essay on the Origins of the Mexican War* (Albuquerque: University of New Mexico Press, 1975).	23
43	Branson, Farrel A., Gerald F. Gifford, Kenneth G. Renard, and Richard F. Hadley. *Rangeland Hydrology* (Dubuque, Iowa: Kendall/Hunt Pub. Co., 2d ed. 1981).	63
44	Briggs, Charles L., and John R. Van Ness. *Land, Water and Culture: New Perspectives on Hispanic Land Grants* (Albuquerque: University of New Mexico, 1987).	43
45	Brown, Bruce. *Mountain in the Clouds: A Search for the Wild Salmon* (New York: Simon & Schuster, 1982).	67
46	Brown, David E. *Arizona Wetlands and Water Fowl* (Tucson: University of Arizona Press, 1985).	70
47	Brown, David E. *The Grizzly in the Southwest: Documentary of an Extinction* (Norman: University of Oklahoma Press, 1985).	66

ITEM	AUTHOR & TITLE	PAGE NO.
48	Brown, David E., ed. *The Wolf in the Southwest: The Making of an Endangered Species* (Tucson: University of Arizona Press, 1983).	67
49	Brown, F. Lee, and Helen M. Ingram. *Water and Poverty in the Southwest* (Tucson: University of Arizona Press, 1987).	30, 85
50	Brown, James Lorin. *The Mussel Slough Tragedy* (n.p., 1958).	25
51	Brown, Leslie. *Eagles of the World* (New York: Universe Books, 1977).	67
52	Buchholtz, C. W. *Rocky Mountain National Park: A History* (Boulder: Colorado Associated University Press, 1983).	30
53	Cafferty, Pastora San Juan, and William C. McCready, eds. *Hispanics in the United States: A New Social Agenda* (New Brunswick, N.J.: Transaction Books, 1985).	24, 42
54	Cahn, Robert. *The Fight to Save Wild Alaska* (Portland: Audubon Society of Portland, 1982).	29
55	California Department of Water Resources. *Water Conservation in California* (Sacramento: State of California, Resources Agency, Dept. of Water Resources, 1984).	63
56	Camarillo, Albert. *Chicanos in a Changing Society* (Cambridge: Harvard University Press, 1979).	42

ITEM	AUTHOR & TITLE	PAGE NO.
57	Caras, Roger. *Monarch of Deadman Bay: The Life and Death of a Kodiak Bear* (Boston: Little, Brown, 1969).	66
58	Carson, Gerald. *Men, Beasts, and Gods: A History of Cruelty and Kindness to Animals* (New York: Scribner's, 1972).	72, 73
59	Carstensen, Vernon Rosco, ed. *The Public Lands: Studies in the History of the Public Domain* (Madison: University of Wisconsin Press, 1962)	24
60	Cather, Willa. *O Pioneers!* (Boston: Houghton Mifflin, 1988; orig. pub., 1913).	55
61	Cather, Willa. *My Antonia* (Boston: Houghton Mifflin, 1954; orig. pub., 1918).	55
62	Cather, Willa. *Death Comes for the Archbishop* (New York: Knopf, 1927).	43
63	Chase, Alston. *Playing God in Yellowstone: The Destruction of America's First National Park* (Boston: Atlantic Monthly Press, 1986).	58
64	Chen, Jack. *The Chinese of America* (New York: Harper & Row, 1980).	45
65	Childerhose, R. J., and Marj Trim. *Pacific Salmon and Steelhead Trout* (Seattle: University of Washington Press, 1979).	67
66	Chittenden, Hiram Martin. *The American Fur Trade of the Far West* (Stanford, Calif.: Academic Reprints, 1902 & photo reprint 1954) (two volumes).	51

ITEM	AUTHOR & TITLE	PAGE NO.
67	Clappe, Louise Amelia Knapp Smith. *The Shirley Letters from the California Mines, 1851–1852* (New York: Ballantine Books, 1971; orig. pub., 1854–55).	16, 83
68	Clark, Walter Van Tilburg. *The City of Trembling Leaves* (New York: Random House, 1945).	57
69	Clark, Walter Van Tilburg. *The Track of the Cat* (New York: Random House, 1949).	57
70	Clarkson, Ewan. *Wolf Country: A Wilderness Pilgrimage* (New York: Dutton, 1975).	67
71	Clawson, Marion. *Forests for Whom and for What?* (Baltimore: Johns Hopkins University Press, 1975).	64, 80
72	Cleland, Robert. *This Reckless Breed of Men: The Trappers and Fur Traders of the Southwest* (New York: Knopf, 1950).	34
73	Cline, Gloria Griffen. *Exploring the Great Basin* (Norman: University of Oklahoma Press, 1963).	57
74	Clyman, James. *James Clyman, American Frontiersman, 1792–1881: The Adventures of a Trapper and Covered Wagon Emigrant as Told in His Own Reminiscences and Diaries*, Charles L. Camp, ed. (Portland, Oreg.: Champoeg Press, 1960) (Camp, Charles L., ed.).	51
75	Coggins, George Cameron, and Deborah Lyndall Smith. "The Emerging Law of Wildlife: A Narrative Bibliography," *Environmental Law*, volume 6, at p. 583 (1975).	68

ITEM	AUTHOR & TITLE	PAGE NO.
76	Coggins, George Cameron, and Sebastian T. Patti. "The Emerging Law of Wildlife II: A Narrative Bibliography of Federal Wildlife Law," *Harvard Environmental Law Review*, volume 4, at p. 164 (1980).	68
77	Coggins, George Cameron, and Charles F. Wilkinson. *Federal Public Land & Resources Law* (Mineloa, N.Y.: Foundation Press, 2d ed. 1987).	51, 77
78	Cohen, Fay G. *Treaties on Trial: The Continuing Controversy over Northwest Indian Fishing Rights* (Seattle: University of Washington Press, 1986).	81
79	Cohen, Michael P. *The Pathless Way: John Muir and the American Wilderness* (Madison: University of Wisconsin Press, 1984).	36
80	Cohen, Michael P. *The History of the Sierra Club, 1892–1970* (San Francisco: Sierra Club Books, 1988).	50
81	Collier, John. *The Indians of the Americas* (New York: W. W. Norton, 1947).	37
82	Collier, John. "The Genesis and Philosophy of the Reorganization Act" in *Indian Affairs and the Indian Reorganization Act, The Twenty Year Record*, at p. 2 (William H. Kelly, ed. Tucson: University of Arizona Press, 1954).	37, 38

ITEM	AUTHOR & TITLE	PAGE NO.
83	Conservation Foundation. *Forest Land Use: An Annotated Bibliography of Policy, Economics, and Management Issues, 1970–1980* (compiled by William E. Shands) (Washington, D.C.: The Foundation, 1981).	65
84	Corle, Edwin. *Listen, Bright Angel* (New York: Duell, Sloan & Pearce, 1946).	54
85	Corle, Edwin. *The Gila: River of the Southwest* (Lincoln: University of Nebraska Press, 1951).	55
86	Craighead, Frank C., Jr. *Track of the Grizzly* (San Francisco: Sierra Club Books, 1979).	58, 66
87	Dana, Richard Henry. *Two Years Before the Mast: a Personal Narrative of Life at Sea* (New York: Penguin Books, 1981; orig. pub., 1911).	16
88	Dana, Samuel T., and Sally K. Fairfax. *Forest and Range Policy* (New York: McGraw-Hill, 2d ed. 1980).	14, 47, 77
89	Daniel, Cletus E. *Bitter Harvest: A History of California Farmworkers, 1870–1941* (Ithaca, N.Y.: Cornell University Press, 1981).	45
90	Daniel, T., J. Helms, and Frederick Storrs Baker. *Principles of Silviculture* (New York: McGraw-Hill, 2d ed. 1979).	64
91	Dasmann, Raymond F. *Environmental Conservation* (New York: Wiley, 5th ed. 1984).	79
92	Debo, Angie. *The Road to Disappearance* (Norman: University of Oklahoma Press, 1941).	23

BIBLIOGRAPHY

ITEM	AUTHOR & TITLE	PAGE NO.
93	Debo, Angie. *The Rise and Fall of the Choctaw Republic* (Norman: University of Oklahoma Press, 2d ed. 1961).	23
94	DeBuys, William Eno. *Enchantment and Exploitation: The Life and Hard Times of a New Mexico Mountain Range* (Albuquerque: University of New Mexico Press, 1985).	54
95	Deloria, Vine, Jr. *Custer Died for Your Sins: An Indian Manifesto* (New York: Macmillan, 1969).	9, 41
96	Deloria, Vine, Jr., and Clifford M. Lytle. *The Nations Within: The Past and Future of American Indian Sovereignty* (New York: Pantheon Books, 1984).	81
97	DeVoto, Bernard. *The Year of Decision: 1846* (Boston: Little Brown, 1943).	9, 15, 43
98	DeVoto, Bernard. *Across the Wide Missouri* (Boston: Houghton Mifflin, 1947).	16, 34, 67
99	DeVoto, Bernard. *The Course of Empire* (Boston: Houghton Mifflin, 1952).	15
100	DeVoto, Bernard. *The Journals of Lewis & Clark* (Boston: Houghton Mifflin, 1953).	33
101	Dick, Everett. *The Lure of the Land: A Social History of the Public Lands from the Articles of Confederation to the New Deal* (Lincoln: University of Nebraska Press, 1970).	17
102	Dippie, Brian W. *The Vanishing American: White Attitudes and U.S. Indian Policy* (Middletown, Conn.: Wesleyan University Press, 1982).	30, 81

ITEM	AUTHOR & TITLE	PAGE NO.
103	Doig, Ivan. *This House of Sky: Landscapes of a Western Mind* (San Diego: Harcourt Brace Jovanovich, 1978).	45
104	Doig, Ivan. *English Creek* (New York: Atheneum, 1984).	45, 47
105	Doig, Ivan. *Dancing at the Rascal Fair* (New York: Atheneum, 1987).	45
106	Dorn, Edward. *Slinger* (Berkeley: Wingbow, 1975).	72
107	Dott, R. H., Jr., and R. L. Batten. *Evolution of the Earth* (New York: McGraw-Hill, 4th ed. 1987).	62
108	Drago, Harry S. *The Great Range Wars: Violence on the Grasslands* (New York: Dodd, Mead, 1970).	26
109	Dunbar, Robert G. *Forging New Rights in Western Waters* (Lincoln: University of Nebraska Press, 1983).	10, 20
110	Duncan, David J. *The River Why* (San Francisco: Sierra Club Books, 1983).	72
111	Durham, Philip, and Everett L. Jones. *The Negro Cowboys* (New York: Dodd, Mead & Co., 1965).	51
112	Ehrlich, Gretel. *To Touch the Water* (Boise, Id.: Ahsahta Press, 1981).	51
113	Ehrlich, Gretel. *The Solace of Open Spaces* (New York: Viking Press, 1985).	45, 46, 51

BIBLIOGRAPHY

ITEM	AUTHOR & TITLE	PAGE NO.

114   Eicher, Don L. *Geologic Time* (Englewood Cliffs, N.J.: Prentice-Hall, 2d ed. 1976).   84

115   Elston, Allan Vaughan. *The Marked Men* (Philadelphia: Lippincott,1956).   26

116   Engelbert, Ernest A., ed. with Ann Foley Scheuring. *Water Scarcity: Impacts on Western Agriculture* (Berkeley: University of California Press, 1984).   63

117   Environmental Defense Fund. *Trading Conservation Investments for Water* (Berkeley: Environmental Defense Fund, Inc., 1983).   80

118   *Environmental Ethics.* (A quarterly publication of the John Muir Institute for Environmental Studies, Inc. and the University of New Mexico; Department of Philosophy, University of New Mexico, Albuquerque, NM 87131).   79

119   Erdrich, Louise. *Love Medicine* (New York: Holt, Rinehart, and Winston, 1984).   41, 55

120   Erdrich, Louise. *The Beet Queen* (New York: Holt, Rinehart, and Winston, 1986).   41, 55

121   Etherington, John R. *Wetland Ecology* (New York: State Mutual Book & Periodical Service, Ltd., 1983).   70

122   Faragher, John M. *Women and Men on the Overland Trail* (New Haven: Yale University Press, 1979).   83

ITEM	AUTHOR & TITLE	PAGE NO.
123	Favour, Alpheus H. *Old Bill Williams: Mountain Man* (Norman: University of Oklahoma Press, rev. ed. 1962).	50
124	Ferber, Edna. *So Big* (Garden City, N.Y.: Doubleday, Page, & Co., 1924).	55
125	Ferber, Edna. *Great Son* (Garden City, N.Y.: Doubleday, 1945).	55
126	Ferguson, Denzel, and Nancy Ferguson. *Sacred Cows at the Public Trough* (Bend, Oreg.: Maverick Publications, 1983).	64
127	Fitzharris, Tim. *The Wild Prairie: A Natural History of the Western Plains* (Toronto: Oxford University Press, 1983).	55, 72
128	Folk-Williams, John A., Susan Fry, and Lucy Hilgendorf. *Western Water Flows to the Cities* (Santa Fe, N.M.: Western Network, Covelo, Calif.: Island Press, 1985).	63
129	Folk-Williams, John A., and Steven J. Shupe. *The Rio Grande* (Santa Fe: Western Network, 1988).	54
130	Foote, Mary Hallock. *A Victorian Gentlewoman in the Far West: The Reminiscences of Mary Hallock Foote* (Rodman Paul, ed.) (San Marino, Calif.: Huntington Library, 1983; orig. pub. 1972).	83
131	Foreman, Grant. *Indian Removal: The Emigration of the Five Civilized Tribes of Indians* (Norman: University of Oklahoma Press, 1953).	23

ITEM	AUTHOR & TITLE	PAGE NO.
132	Foss, Philip O. *Politics and Grass: The Administration of Grazing on the Public Domain* (New York: Greenwood Press, 1960).	18
133	Fox, Stephen. *John Muir and His Legacy: The American Conservation Movement* (Boston: Little, Brown, 1981).	36, 50
134	Fradkin, Philip L. *A River No More: The Colorado River and the West* (New York: Knopf, 1981).	21, 29, 54
135	Fritz, Henry E. *The Movement for Indian Assimilation 1860 to 1890* (Philadelphia: University of Pennsylvania Press, 1963).	20
136	Garland, Hamlin. *A Son of the Middle Border* (New York: Macmillan, 1917).	17, 55
137	Garland, Hamlin. *A Daughter of the Middle Border* (New York: Macmillan, 1921).	17, 55
138	Gates, Paul W., with a chapter by Robert W. Swenson. *History of Public Land Law Development* (Washington, D.C.: U.S. Govt. Print. Off.; for sale by the Supt. of Docs., 1968).	14
139	Gilbert, Bil. *Westering Man: The Life of Joseph Walker* (New York: Atheneum, 1983).	50
140	Gilliam, Ann, ed. *Voices for the Earth: A Treasury of the Sierra Club Bulletin* (San Francisco: Sierra Club Books, 1979).	50
141	Gilliam, Harold. *Weather of the San Francisco Bay Region* (Berkeley: University of California Press, 1962).	59

ITEM	AUTHOR & TITLE	PAGE NO.
142	Glasscock, Carl Burgess. *The War of the Copper Kings; Builders of Butte and Wolves of Wall Street* (New York: Bobbs-Merrill, 1935).	35
143	Gottlieb, Robert, and Peter Wiley. *America's Saints: The Rise of Mormon Power* (New York: G. P. Putnam, 1984).	44
144	*Great Plains Quarterly*. (Center for Great Plains Studies, University of Nebraska–Lincoln; 1214 Oldfather Hall, University of Nebraska–Lincoln, Lincoln, NE 68588).	56
145	Greever, William S. *The Bonanza West: The Story of the Western Mining Rushes, 1848–1900* (Norman: University of Oklahoma Press, 1963).	16
146	Gruening, Ernest Henry. *The Battle for Alaska Statehood* (College: University of Alaska Press, distributed by the University of Washington Press, Seattle, 1967).	28
147	Guthrie, Alfred B., Jr. *The Big Sky* (Alexandria, Va.: Time-Life Books Inc., 1980; orig. pub., 1947).	34
148	Guthrie, Alfred B., Jr. *The Way West* (New York: William Sloane, 1949).	15
149	Guthrie, Woody. *Bound for Glory* (New York: Dutton, 1943).	17
150	Hafen, Le Roy R. *Broken Hand: The Life of Thomas Fitzpatrick, Mountain Man, Guide, and Indian Agent* (Denver, Colo.: Old West Pub. Co., rev. ed. 1973).	50

ITEM	AUTHOR & TITLE	PAGE NO.
151	Hafen, Le Roy R. *Mountain Men and Fur Traders of the Far West: Eighteen Biographical Sketches* (Lincoln: University of Nebraska Press, 1982).	51
152	Hafen, Le Roy R. *Trappers of the Far West: Sixteen Biographical Sketches* (Lincoln: University of Nebraska Press, 1983).	51
153	Hafen, Le Roy R., ed. *The Mountain Men and the Fur Trade of the Far West* (Glendale, Calif.: A. H. Clark Co., 1965) (ten volumes).	51
154	Haines, Aubrey L. *The Yellowstone Story: A History of Our First National Park* (Yellowstone National Park, Wyo.: Yellowstone Library and Museum Assoc. in cooperation with the Colorado Associated University Press, 1977) (two volumes).	30, 58
155	Hardin, Garrett. "The Tragedy of the Commons," *Science*, volume 162, at p. 1243 (1968).	76
156	Harris, Larry D. *The Fragmented Forest: Island Biogeography Theory and the Preservation of Biotic Diversity* (Chicago: University of Chicago Press, 1984).	69
157	Harrison, Jim. *Legends of the Fall* (New York: Delacorte Press/ S. Lawrence, 1979).	46
158	Harth, D., and L. Baldwin. *Voices of Aztlan: Chicano Literature of Today* (New York: New American Library, 1974).	43
159	Hasselstrom, Linda M., ed. *James Clyman, Journal of a Mountain Man* (Missoula, Mont.: Mountain Press Pub. Co., 1984).	51

ITEM	AUTHOR & TITLE	PAGE NO.
160	Hays, Hoffman Reynolds. *Children of the Raven: The Seven Indian Nations of the Northwest Coast* (New York: McGraw-Hill, 1975).	59
161	Hays, Samuel P. *Conservation and the Gospel of Efficiency: The Progressive Conservation Movement, 1890–1920* (Cambridge: Harvard University Press, 1959).	9, 37, 77
162	Hays, Samuel P. *Beauty, Health, and Permanence: Environmental Politics in the United States, 1955–1985* (Cambridge, N.Y.: Cambridge University Press, 1987).	50
163	Heady, Harold F. *Rangeland Management* (New York: McGraw-Hill, 1975).	63
164	Hedgpeth, Joel W. *Introduction to Seashore Life of the San Francisco Bay Region and the Coast of Northern California* (Berkeley: University of California Press, 1962).	59
165	Heinerman, John, and Anson Shupe. *The Mormon Corporate Empire* (Boston: Beacon Press, 1985).	44, 51
166	Hendee, John C., George H. Stankey, and Robert C. Lucas. *Wilderness Management* (Washington, D.C.: Forest Service, U.S. Dept. of Agriculture, U.S. Govt. Print. Off., 1978).	78
167	Henderson, Randall. *Sun, Sand and Solitude: Vignettes from the Notebook of a Veteran Desert Reporter* (Los Angeles: Westernlore Press, 1968).	54

BIBLIOGRAPHY

ITEM	AUTHOR & TITLE	PAGE NO.
168	Hidy, Ralph Willard, Frank Ernest Hill, and Allan Nevins. *Timber and Men: The Weyerhauser Story* (New York: Macmillan, 1963).	49
169	High Country News. *Western Water Made Simple* (Washington, D.C., Covelo, Calif.: Island Press, 1987).	63
170	*High Country News* (A biweekly publication of the High Country News Foundation, Box 1090, 124 Grand Avenue, Paonia, CO 81428).	9
171	Hillerman, Tony. *The Dark Wind* (New York: Harper & Row, 1982).	48
172	Hoffman, Abraham. *Vision or Villainy: Origins of the Owens Valley-Los Angeles Water Controversy* (College Station: Texas A & M University Press, 1981).	27
173	Hofstadter, Richard, and Seymour Martin Lipset, eds. *Turner and the Sociology of the Frontier* (New York: Basic Books, 1968).	13
174	Holbrook, Stewart Hall. *The Columbia* (New York: Rinehart, 1956).	54
175	Holliday, J. S. *The World Rushed In: The California Gold Rush Experience* (New York: Simon and Schuster, 1981).	16
176	Holthaus, Gary H. *Circling Back* (Salt Lake City: G. M. Smith, 1984).	33
177	Horgan, Paul. *Great River: The Rio Grande in North American History* (New York: Rinehart, 1954) (two volumes).	54

ITEM	AUTHOR & TITLE	PAGE NO.
178	Horwitz, Eleanor C. J., ed. *Clearcutting: A View From the Top* (Washington: Acropolis Books, 1974).	65
179	Houghton, Samuel Gilbert. *A Trace of Desert Waters: The Great Basin Story* (Glendale, Calif.: A. H. Clarke Co., 1976).	57
180	Hoxie, Frederick E. *A Final Promise: The Campaign to Assimilate the Indians, 1880–1920* (Lincoln: University of Nebraska Press, 1984).	19
181	Hugo, Richard F. *The Lady in Kicking Horse Reservoir* (New York: Norton, 1973).	72
182	Hugo, Richard F. *What Thou Lovest Well, Remains American* (New York: Norton, 1975).	72
183	Hundley, Norris, Jr. *Water and the West: The Colorado River Compact and the Politics of Water in the American West* (Berkeley: University of California Press, 1975).	54
184	Hutchins, Wells A. "The Community Acequia: Its Origin and Development," *Southwestern Historical Quarterly*, volume 31, at p. 261 (1928).	86
185	Irving, Washington. *The Adventures of Captain Bonneville, U.S.A., in the Rocky Mountains and the Far West* (New York: G. P. Putnam, rev. ed. 1849).	33
186	Irving, Washington. *Astoria, or Anecdotes of an Enterprise Beyond the Rocky Mountains* (ed. Richard Dilworth Rust, Boston: Twayne Publishers, 1976; orig. pub. 1868).	33

ITEM	AUTHOR & TITLE	PAGE NO.
187	Ise, John. *Our National Parks Policy—A Critical History* (Baltimore: Published for Resources for the Future by Johns Hopkins University Press, 1961).	30
188	Iverson, Peter. *The Navajo Nation* (Westport, Conn.: Greenwood Press, 1981).	48
189	Jackson, Helen Hunt. *A Century of Dishonor: A Sketch of the United States Government's Dealings with Some of the Indian Tribes* (Williamstown, Mass.: Corner House, 1979; orig. pub., 1881).	23
190	Jeffrey, Julie R. *Frontier Women: The Trans-Mississippi West, 1840–1880* (New York: Hill & Wang, 1979).	83
191	Johnsgard, Paul A. *Water Fowl of North America* (Bloomington: Indiana University Press, 1975).	70
192	Jones, Holway R. *John Muir and the Sierra Club: The Battle for Yosemite* (San Francisco: Sierra Club, 1965).	27, 36, 50
193	Jordan, Teresa. *Cowgirls: Women of the American West* (New York: Anchor Books, 1982).	51
194	Josephy, Alvin M., Jr. *The Nez Perce Indians and the Opening of the Northwest* (New Haven: Yale University Press, 1965).	23
195	*Journal of the West*, volume 24, No. 1, "Law in the West" (1985).	10

ITEM	AUTHOR & TITLE	PAGE NO.
196	Julian, George W. *Political Recollections, 1840 to 1872* (Chicago: Jansen, McClurg, & Co., 1883).	17
197	Kahrl, William L. *Water and Power: The Conflict over Los Angeles' Water Supply in the Owens Valley* (Berkeley: University of California Press, 1982).	27
198	Kahrl, William L., ed., and California State Office of Planning and Research. *The California Water Atlas* (Sacramento: The Governor's Office of Planning and Research, 1979).	62
199	Katz, William Loren, *The Black West* (Garden City: N.Y.: Anchor Press/ Doubleday, 1973).	51
200	Kaufman, Herbert. *The Forest Ranger: A Study in Administrative Behavior* (Baltimore: Published for Resources for the Future by Johns Hopkins University Press, 1960).	47
201	Kelley, Robert L. *Gold vs. Grain: The Hydraulic Mining Controversy in California's Sacramento Valley* (Glendale, Calif.: A. H. Clark Co., 1959).	76
202	Kelly, Lawrence C. *The Navajo Indians and Federal Indian Policy, 1900-1935* (Tucson: University of Arizona Press, 1968).	48
203	Kelly, Lawrence C. *The Assault on Assimilation: John Collier and the Origins of Indian Policy Reform* (Albuquerque: University of New Mexico Press, 1983).	37
204	Kemmis, Dan. *Community on the Frontier* (Norman: University of Oklahoma Press, forthcoming).	83

ITEM	AUTHOR & TITLE	PAGE NO.
205	Kerouac, Jack. *On the Road* (New York: New American Library, 1957).	72
206	Kerouac, Jack. *The Dharma Bums* (New York: Viking Press, 1958).	72
207	Kesey, Ken. *One Flew Over the Cuckoo's Nest* (New York: Viking Press, 1962).	27
208	Kesey, Ken. *Sometimes a Great Notion* (New York: Bantam Books, 1963).	46
209	Kingston, Maxine H. *The Woman Warrior: Memoirs of a Girlhood Among Ghosts* (New York: Vintage Books, 1977).	45
210	Kingston, Maxine H. *China Men* (New York: Knopf, 1980).	45
211	Kinney, Jay. P. *A Continent Lost, A Civilization Won: Indian Land Tenure in America* (Baltimore: Johns Hopkins University Press, 1937).	19
212	Kiser, George C., and Martha Woody Kiser, eds. *Mexican Workers in the United States: Historical and Political Perspectives* (Albuquerque: University of New Mexico Press, 1979).	24, 42
213	Kittredge, William. *We Are Not in This Together: Stories* (Port Townsend, Wash.: Graywolf Press, 1984).	72
214	Kittredge, William. *Owning It All: Essays* (Saint Paul, Minn.: Graywolf Press, 1987).	3, 9, 72, 76

ITEM	AUTHOR & TITLE	PAGE NO.
215	Kittredge, William, and Annick Smith. *The Last Best Place, A Montana Anthology* (Helena: Montana Historical Society, 1988).	71
216	Knack, Martha C., and Omer C. Stewart. *As Long as the River Shall Run: An Ethnohistory of Pyramid Lake Indian Reservation* (Berkeley: University of California Press, 1984).	57
217	Kneese, Allen, and F. Lee Brown. *The Southwest Under Stress: National Resource Development Issues in a Regional Setting* (Baltimore: Published for Resources for the Future by the Johns Hopkins University Press, 1981).	80
218	Knoll, Tricia. *Becoming Americans: Asian Sojourners, Immigrants, and Refugees in the Western United States* (Portland, Oreg.: Coast to Coast Books, 1982).	45
219	Kraenzel, Carl F. *The Great Plains in Transition* (Norman: University of Oklahoma Press, 1955).	56
220	Lamm, Richard D., and Michael McCarthy. *The Angry West: A Vulnerable Land and Its Future* (Boston: Houghton Mifflin, 1982).	22, 29, 30, 39
221	Lange, Dorothea, and Paul S. Taylor. *An American Exodus: A Record of Human Erosion* (New Haven: Published for the Oakland Museum by Yale University Press, 1969).	17
222	Larson, Edwin E., and Peter W. Birkeland, eds. *Putnam's Geology* (New York: Oxford University Press, 4th ed. 1982).	62

ITEM	AUTHOR & TITLE	PAGE NO.
223	Lavender, David Sievert. *Bent's Fort* (Garden City, N.Y.: Dolphin Books, Doubleday & Co., 1954).	34
224	Lavender, David Sievert. *The Rockies* (New York: Harper & Row, 1975).	34
225	Laxalt, Robert. *Sweet Promised Land* (New York: Harper & Row, 1957).	57
226	Laycock, George. *Autumn of the Eagle* (New York: Scribner's, 1973).	67
227	Le Master, Dennis C. *Decade of Change: The Remaking of Forest Service Statutory Authority During the 1970's* (Westport, Conn.: Greenword Press, 1984).	47
228	Lecomber, Richard. *The Economics of Natural Resources* (New York: Wiley, 1979).	80
229	Leopold, A. Starker, Ralph J. Gutierrez, and Michael T. Bronson. *North American Game Birds and Mammals* (New York: Scribner's, 1981).	72
230	Leopold, A. Starker, and Tupper Ansel Blake. *Wild California: Vanishing Lands, Vanishing Wildlife* (Berkeley: University of California Press, 1985).	68, 73
231	Leopold, Aldo. *Game Management* (New York: C. Scribner's, 1933).	68, 77
232	Leopold, Aldo. *A Sand County Almanac, with Other Essays on Conservation from Round River* (New York: Oxford University Press, 1966; orig. pub., 1949).	9, 72, 78, 79, 85

ITEM	AUTHOR & TITLE	PAGE NO.
233	Leshy, John D. *The Mining Law: A Study in Perpetual Motion* (Washington, D.C.: Resources for the Future, Inc., 1987).	10, 29, 76
234	Lewis, Oscar. *The Big Four: The Story of Huntington, Stanford, Hopkins and Crocker, and of the Building of the Central Pacific* (New York: Knopf, 1938).	25, 34
235	Lewis, Oscar, and Carroll D. Hall. *Bonanza Inn: America's First Luxury Hotel* (New York: Knopf, 1939).	35
236	Libecap, Gary D. *Locking Up the Range: Federal Land Controls and Grazing* (San Francisco: Pacific Institute for Public Policy Research, 1981).	63
237	*Light v. United States*, 220 U.S. 523 (1911).	51
238	Limerick, Patricia Nelson. *Desert Passages: Encounters with the American Deserts* (Albuquerque: University of New Mexico Press, 1985).	57
239	Limerick, Patricia Nelson. *Legacy of Conquest: The Unbroken Past of the American West* (New York: Norton, 1987).	14, 22, 29
240	Lingenfelter, Richard E. *The Hardrock Miners: A History of the Mining Labor Movement in the American West, 1863–1893* (Berkeley: University of California Press, 1974).	16
241	Llewellyn, Karl N., and E. Adamson Hoebel. *The Cheyenne Way* (Norman: University of Oklahoma Press, 1941).	81

ITEM	AUTHOR & TITLE	PAGE NO.
242	London, Jack. *The Son of the Wolf: Tales of the Far North* (New York: Grosset & Dunlap, 1900).	60
243	London, Jack. *Call of the Wild* (New York: Harmony Books, 1977; orig. pub., 1903).	60
244	London, Jack. *The Sea Wolf* (New York: Macmillan, 1904).	59
245	London, Jack. *White Fang and Selected Stories* (New York: New American Library, 1964; orig. pub., 1906).	60
246	Lopez, Barry H. *Of Wolves and Men* (New York: Scribner's, 1978).	67
247	Lopez, Barry H. *Arctic Dreams: Imagination and Desire in a Northern Landscape* (New York: Scribner's, 1986).	59
248	Love, John. *The Return of the Sea Eagle* (Cambridge: University Press, 1983).	67
249	Luchetti, Cathy, and Carol Olwell. *Women of the West* (St. George, Utah: Antelope Island Press, 1982).	83
250	Lyman, George Dunlap. *The Saga of the Comstock Lode: Boom Days in Virginia City, Nevada* (New York: Scribner's, 1934).	35
251	Lyman, George Dunlap. *Ralston's Ring: California Plunders the Comstock Lode* (New York: Scribner's, 1937).	35

ITEM	AUTHOR & TITLE	PAGE NO.
252	MacLean, Norman. *A River Runs Through It and Other Stories* (Chicago: University of Chicago Press, 1976).	46, 72
253	Marshall, Robert. *Arctic Village* (New York: H. Smith and R. Haas, 1933).	60
254	Marshall, Robert. (George Marshall, ed.) *Arctic Wilderness* (Berkeley: University of California Press, 1956).	60
255	Marshall, Robert. *Alaska Wilderness: Exploring the Central Brooks Range* (Berkeley: University of California Press, 1970; orig. pub., 1956).	60
256	Martin, Russell, and Marc Barasch, eds. *Writers of the Purple Sage: An Anthology of Recent Western Writing* (New York: Viking Press, 1984).	71, 73
257	Martin, William E., Helen M. Ingram, Nancy K. Laney, and Adrian H. Griffin. *Saving Water in a Desert City* (Washington, D.C.: Resources for the Future, Baltimore: Distributed by Johns Hopkins University Press, 1984).	80
258	Maser, Chris. *The Redesigned Forest* (San Pedro, Calif.: R. & E. Miles, 1988).	69
259	Matthiessen, Peter. *Wildlife in America* (New York: Viking Press, 1987; orig. pub., 1959).	73
260	Matthiessen, Peter. *Indian Country* (New York: Viking Press, 1984).	38

ITEM	AUTHOR & TITLE	PAGE NO.
261	McCall, Tom, and Steve Neal. *Tom McCall: Maverick: An Autobiography* (Portland, Oreg.: Binford & Mort, 1977).	39
262	McConnaughey, Bayard, and Evelyn McConnaughey. *Pacific Coast* (New York: Knopf, 1985).	59
263	McGinniss, Joe. *Going to Extremes* (New York: Knopf, 1980).	59
264	McGuane, Thomas. *Nobody's Angel* (New York: Random House, 1981).	46
265	McMurtry, Larry. *Lonesome Dove* (New York: Simon & Schuster, 1985).	26
266	McNamee, Thomas. *The Grizzly Bear* (New York: Knopf, 1984).	66
267	McNickle, D'Arcy. *They Came Here First: The Epic of the American Indian* (New York: Octagon Books, rev. ed. 1975).	41
268	McPhee, John. *Encounters with the Archdruid* (New York: Farrar, Straus, and Giroux, 1971).	20
269	McPhee, John. *Coming into the Country* (New York: Farrar, Straus, and Giroux, 1977).	9, 29, 59
270	McPhee, John. *Basin and Range* (New York: Farrar, Straus, and Giroux, 1981).	9, 56, 84, 85, 86
271	McPhee, John. *Rising from the Plains* (New York: Farrar, Straus, and Giroux, 1986).	85

ITEM	AUTHOR & TITLE	PAGE NO.
272	McPherren, Ida Geneva Miller. *Trail's End* (Casper, Wyo.: Prairie Publishing Co., 1938).	26
273	McWilliams, Carey. *North from Mexico: The Spanish Speaking People of the United States* (New York: Greenwood Press, 1968).	24, 42
274	Mech, L. David. *The Wolf: The Ecology and Behavior of an Endangered Species* (Garden City, N.Y.: Published for the American Museum of Natural History by the Natural History Press, 1970).	67
275	Mercer, A. S. *The Banditti of the Plains* (Norman: University of Oklahoma Press, 1954).	26
276	Meyer, Michael C. *Water in the Hispanic Southwest: A Social and Legal History, 1550–1850* (Tucson: University of Arizona Press, 1984).	54, 85
277	Miller, May Merrill. *First the Blade* (New York: Knopf, 1938).	30
278	Momaday, N. Scott. *House Made of Dawn* (New York: New American Library, 1969).	41
279	Morgan, Dale L. *Jedediah Smith and the Opening of the West* (Indianapolis: Bobbs-Merrill, 1953).	34
280	Morgan, Dale L., ed. *The West of William H. Ashley, 1822–1838* (Denver: Old West Pub. Co., 1964).	34
281	Mowat, Farley. *Never Cry Wolf* (New York: Bantam Books, 1973).	67

ITEM	AUTHOR & TITLE	PAGE NO.
282	Mueller, Jerry E. *Restless River: International Law and the Behavior of the Rio Grande* (El Paso: Texas Western Press, 1975).	54
283	Muir, John. *Our National Parks* (Boston: Houghton Mifflin, 1901).	36
284	Muir, John. *Stickeen: The Story of a Dog* (Boston: Houghton Mifflin, 1909).	51
285	Muir, John. *My First Summer in the Sierra* (Boston: Houghton Mifflin, 1911).	36
286	Muir, John. *The Mountains of California* (New York: The Century Co., rev. ed. 1911).	36
287	Muir, John. *The Story of My Boyhood and Youth* (Madison: University of Wisconsin Press, 1965; orig. pub., 1913).	36
288	Muir, John. *Travels in Alaska* (San Francisco: Sierra Club Books, 1988; orig. pub., 1915).	36, 60
289	Murie, Adolph. *The Wolves of Mount McKinley* (Washington, D.C.: U.S. Govt. Print. Off., 1944).	67
290	Murie, Adolph. *A Naturalist in Alaska* (New York: Devin-Adair Co., 1961).	60, 72
291	Murie, Margaret E. *Two in the Far North* (Anchorage: Alaska Northwest Pub. Co., 2d ed. 1978).	60
292	Murie, Margaret E. *Wapiti Wilderness* (with pen-and-ink drawings by Olaus Murie) (Boulder: Colorado Associated University Press, 1985).	58

ITEM	AUTHOR & TITLE	PAGE NO.
293	Murie, Olaus Johan. *The Elk of North America* (Harrisburg, Pa.: Stackpole Co., 1951).	60
294	Murie, Olaus Johan. *Journeys to the Far North* (Palo Alto, Calif.: American West Pub. Co., 1973).	60
295	Murie, Olaus Johan. *The Alaskan Bird Sketches of Olaus Murie: With Excerpts from His Field Notes* (Anchorage: Alaska Northwest Pub. Co., 1979).	60
296	Myres, Sandra L. *Westering Women and the Frontier Experience, 1800–1915* (Albuquerque: University of New Mexico Press, 1982).	82, 86
297	Nadeau, Remi A. *The Water Seekers* (Garden City, N.Y.: Doubleday, 1950).	27
298	Nash, Gerald D. *The American West Transformed: The Impact of the Second World War* (Bloomington: Indiana University Press, 1985).	22
299	Nash, Roderick. *Wilderness and the American Mind* (New Haven, Conn.: Yale University Press, 3d ed. 1982).	9, 19, 28, 78
300	Naske, Claus M. *An Interpretive History of Alaskan Statehood* (Anchorage: Alaska Northwest Pub. Co., 1973).	28
301	Nayman, Jacqueline. *Atlas of Wildlife* (New York: John Day Co., 1972).	72

BIBLIOGRAPHY

ITEM	AUTHOR & TITLE	PAGE NO.
302	Neihardt, John. *Black Elk Speaks : Being the Life Story of a Holy Man of the Oglala Sioux* (Lincoln: University of Nebraska Press, 1979; orig. pub., 1932).	55
303	Neihardt, John. *The Mountain Men: The Song of Three Friends* (Lincoln: University of Nebraska Press, 1971; orig. pub., 1949).	34
304	Nelson, Richard K. *Make Prayers to the Raven: A Koyukon View of the Northern Forest* (Chicago: University of Chicago Press, 1983).	42, 59
305	Netboy, Anthony. *The Columbia River Salmon and Steelhead Trout: Their Fight for Survival* (Seattle: University of Washington Press, 1980).	67
306	Nichols, John. *The Milagro Beanfield War* (New York: Holt, Rinehart, and Winston, 1974).	9, 43
307	Nichols, John. *The Magic Journey* (New York: Holt, Rinehart, and Winston, 1978).	43
308	Nichols, John. *The Nirvana Blues* (New York: Holt, Rinehart, and Winston, 1981).	43
309	Nichols, John. *A Fragile Beauty: John Nichols' Milagro Country* (Salt Lake City: Peregrine Smith Books, 1987).	54
310	Niering, William A. *Wetlands* (New York: Knopf, 1985).	70
311	Norris, Frank. *The Octopus: The Story of California* (New York: Bantam Books, 1958; orig. pub., 1901).	25, 30

ITEM	AUTHOR & TITLE	PAGE NO.
312	North, F. K. *Petroleum Geology* (Boston: Allen & Unwin, 1985).	62
313	Ogden, Gerald. *The United States Forest Service: A Historical Bibliography, 1876-1972* (Davis: Agricultural History Center, University of California, Davis, 1976).	65
314	Otis, D. S. *The Dawes Act and the Allotment of Indian Land* (Norman: University of Oklahoma Press, rev. ed. 1973).	19, 20
315	O'Toole, Randal. *Reforming the Forest Service* (Washington, D.C., Covelo, Calif.: Island Press, 1988).	47, 80
316	Parkman, Francis. *The Oregon Trail: Sketches of Prairie and Rocky-Mountain Life* (Boston: Little, Brown, 1902).	15
317	Parman, Donald L. *The Navajos and the New Deal* (New Haven: Yale University Press, 1976).	48
318	Paul, Rodman Wilson. *California Gold: The Beginning of Mining in the Far West* (Cambridge: Harvard University Press, 1947).	16, 62
319	Paul, Rodman Wilson. *Mining Frontiers of the Far West, 1848-1880* (New York: Holt, Rinehart and Winston, 1963).	16
320	Paz, Octavio. *The Labyrinth of Solitude: Life and Thought in Mexico* (New York: Grove Press, 1961).	24, 42

ITEM	AUTHOR & TITLE	PAGE NO.
321	Peffer, Louise E. *The Closing of the Public Domain: Disposal and Reservation Policies, 1900-50* (Stanford: Stanford University Press, 1951).	18
322	Peters, William C. *Exploration Mining and Geology* (New York: Wiley, 1978).	62
323	Philp, Kenneth R. *John Collier's Crusade for Indian Reform, 1920-1954* (Tucson: University of Arizona Press, 1977).	37
324	Philp, Kenneth R., ed. *Indian Self-Rule: First-Hand Accounts of Indian-White Relations from Roosevelt to Reagan* (Salt Lake City: Howe Bros., 1986).	38
325	Pinchot, Gifford. *The Fight for Conservation* (Seattle: University of Washington Press, 1910).	37, 77
326	Pinchot, Gifford. *Breaking New Ground* (New York: Harcourt, Brace, 1947).	37, 77
327	Pirsig, Robert M. *Zen and the Art of Motorcycle Maintenance: An Inquiry into Values* (New York: W. Morrow, 1974).	72
328	Plowden, David. *Floor of the Sky: The Great Plains* (San Francisco: Sierra Club, 1972).	56
329	Powell, John W. *The Exploration of the Colorado River and Its Canyons* (New York: Dover Publications, 1895 & photo reprint 1961; orig. pub. 1875).	35

ITEM	AUTHOR & TITLE	PAGE NO.
330	Powell, John W. "Report on the Lands of the Arid Region of the United States," Executive Document No. 73, 45th Congress, 2d Session (Cambridge: Belknap Press of Harvard University Press, 1962; orig. pub. 1879).	35
331	Press, Frank, and Raymond Siever. *Earth* (New York: W. H. Freeman, 4th ed. 1986).	62
332	Prucha, Francis Paul. *American Indian Policy in Crisis: Christian Reformers and the Indian, 1865–1900* (Norman: University of Oklahoma Press, 1976).	19, 81
333	Prucha, Francis Paul. *A Bibliographical Guide to the History of Indian-White Relations in the United States* (Chicago: University of Chicago Press, 1977).	xii, 23, 30
334	Prucha, Francis Paul. *United States Indian Policy: A Critical Bibliography* (Bloomington: Published for the Newberry Library by Indiana University Press, 1977).	xii, 23, 30
335	Prucha, Francis Paul. *The Great Father: The United States Government and the American Indians* (Lincoln: University of Nebraska Press, 1984) (two volumes).	23, 30, 81
336	Prucha, Francis Paul. *The Great Father: The United States Government and the American Indians* (Lincoln: University of Nebraska Press, abridged ed. 1986).	23, 30, 81

BIBLIOGRAPHY

ITEM	AUTHOR & TITLE	PAGE NO.
337	Prucha, Francis Paul, ed. *Americanizing the American Indians: Writings by the "Friends of the Indian," 1880–1900* (Cambridge: Harvard University Press, 1973).	20, 81
338	Puter, S. A. *Looters of the Public Domain* (Portland, Oreg.: Portland Printing House, 1908).	17, 18
339	Randolph, Edmund. *Beef, Leather and Grass* (Norman: University of Oklahoma Press, 1981).	51
340	Rea, Amadeo M. *Once a River: Bird Life and Habitat Changes on the Middle Gila* (Tucson: University of Arizona Press, 1983).	70
341	Reid, John Phillip. *A Law of Blood; the Primitive Law of the Cherokee Nation* (New York: New York University Press, 1970).	81
342	Reid, John Phillip. *Law for the Elephant: Property and Social Behavior on the Overland Trail* (San Marino, Calif.: Huntington Library, 1980)	15
343	Reisner, Marc P. *Cadillac Desert: The American West and Its Disappearing Water* (New York: Viking Press, 1986).	9, 21, 27, 29
344	Reese, Rick. *Greater Yellowstone: The National Park and Adjacent Wildlands* (Helena: Montana Magazine, Inc., 1984).	58
345	Richardson, Elmo R. "The Struggle for the Valley: California's Hetch Hetchy Controversy, 1905–1913, "*California Historical Society Quarterly*, volume 38, at p. 249 (1959).	27, 36

ITEM	AUTHOR & TITLE	PAGE NO.
346	Richardson, Elmo R. *Dams, Parks & Politics* (Lexington: University Press of Kentucky, 1973).	28
347	Righter, Robert W. *Crucible for Conservation: The Creation of Grand Teton National Park* (Boulder: Colorado Associated University Press, 1982).	30
348	Robinson, Glen O. *The Forest Service: A Study in Public Land Management* (Baltimore: Published for Resources for the Future by Johns Hopkins University Press, 1975).	47
349	Roca, Paul M. *Paths of the Padres Through Sonora* (Tucson: Arizona Pioneers Historical Society, 1967).	xi
350	Roca, Paul M. *Spanish Jesuit Churches in Mexico's Tarahumara* (Tucson: University of Arizona Press, 1979).	xi
351	Rolston, Holmes, III. *Environmental Ethics: Duties to, and Values in, the Natural World* (Philadelphia: Temple University, 1988)	79
352	Rölvaag, Ole. *Giants in the Earth: A Saga of the Prairie* (New York: Harper, 1927).	17, 55
353	Romo, Ricardo. *East Los Angeles: History of a Barrio* (Austin: University of Texas Press, 1983).	42
354	Roosevelt, Theodore. *Ranch Life and the Hunting-Trail* (New York: The Century Co., 1888).	68
355	Roscow, James P. *800 Miles to Valdez: The Building of the Alaska Pipeline* (Englewood Cliffs, N.J.: Prentice-Hall, 1977).	49

BIBLIOGRAPHY

ITEM	AUTHOR & TITLE	PAGE NO.
356	Runte, Alfred. *National Parks: The American Experience* (Lincoln: University of Nebraska Press, 2d ed. rev., 1987).	30
357	Russell, Osborne. *Journal of a Trapper* (Aubrey L. Haines, ed.) (Lincoln: University of Nebraska Press, 1955; orig. pub., 1921).	51
358	Ruxton, George Frederick Augustus. *Life in the Far West*, Leroy R. Hafen, ed. (Norman: University of Oklahoma Press, 1951; orig. pub., 1849).	51
359	Sale, Kirkpatrick. *Dwellers in the Land: The Bioregional Vision* (San Francisco: Sierra Club Books, 1985).	78
360	Sanchez, George Isidore. *Forgotten People: A Study of New Mexicans* (Albuquerque: C. Horn, 1940).	43
361	Sandoz, Mari. *Crazy Horse: The Strange Man of the Oglalas* (New York: Knopf, 1942).	55
362	Sandoz, Mari. *Cheyenne Autumn* (New York: McGraw-Hill, 1953).	55
363	Sandoz, Mari. *Love Song to the Plains* (New York: Harper, 1961).	56
364	Savage, Arthur, and Candace Savage. *Wild Mammals of Northwest America* (Baltimore: Johns Hopkins University Press, 1981).	72
365	Savage, W. Sherman. *Blacks in the West* (Westport, Conn.: Greenwood Press, 1976).	51

ITEM	AUTHOR & TITLE	PAGE NO.
366	Sax, Joseph L. *Mountains Without Handrails: Reflections on the National Parks* (Ann Arbor: University of Michigan Press, 1980).	19, 30, 78
367	Schlissel, Lillian. *Women's Diaries of the Westward Journey* (New York: Schocken Books, 1982).	83
368	Schullery, Paul. *Mountain Time* (New York: Schocken Books, 1984).	58
369	Schullery, Paul. ed. *Old Yellowstone Days* (Boulder: Colorado Associated University Press, 1979).	58
370	Schultheis, Rob. *The Hidden West: Journeys in the American Outback* (New York: Random House, 1982).	57
371	Service, Robert. "The Cremation of Sam McGee," in *The Spell of the Yukon* (New York: Dodd, Mead, 2d ed. 1916).	60, 72
372	Seton, Ernest T. *The Biography of a Grizzly* (New York: The Century Co., 1900).	66
373	Shankland, Robert. *Steve Mather of the National Parks* (New York: Knopf, 1951).	30
374	Shanks, Bernard. *This Land Is Your Land: The Struggle to Save America's Public Lands* (San Francisco: Sierra Club Books, 1984).	29
375	Sheridan, David. *Desertification in the United States* (Washington, D.C.: Council on Environmental Quality; for sale by the Supt. of Docs. U.S. Govt. Pub. Off., 1981).	63

ITEM	AUTHOR & TITLE	PAGE NO.
376	Shupe, Steven J. "Waste in Western Water Law: A Blueprint for Change," *Oregon Law Review*, volume 61, at p. 483 (1982).	63
377	Sigler, William F. *Wildlife Law Enforcement* (Dubuque, Iowa: W. C. Brown, 3d ed. 1980).	68
378	Silko, Leslie M. *Ceremony* (New York: Viking Press, 1977).	41
379	Silko, Leslie M. *Storyteller* (New York: Seaver Books, distributed by Grove Press, 1981).	41
380	Skinner, Brian J. *Earth Resources* (Englewood Cliffs, N.J.: Prentice-Hall, 3d ed. 1986).	62
381	Slotkin, Richard. *The Fatal Environment: The Myth of the Frontier in the Age of Industrialization, 1800–1890* (New York: Atheneum, 1985).	29
382	Smith, Courtland L. *Salmon Fishers of the Columbia* (Corvallis: Oregon State University Press, 1979).	67
383	Smith, David M. *The Practice of Silviculture* (New York: Wiley, 8th ed. 1986).	64
384	Smith, Helena Huntington. *The War on Powder River* (New York: McGraw-Hill, 1966).	26
385	Smith, Henry Nash. *Virgin Land: The American West as Symbol and Myth* (Cambridge: Harvard University Press, 1950).	14
386	Smythe, William E. *The Conquest of Arid America* (New York: Macmillan, 1905).	20

ITEM	AUTHOR & TITLE	PAGE NO.

387   Snively, Susan. "For the Thirteenth Wife (Susan-Snively, 13th Wife of Brigham Young)" in *From This Distance; Poems* (Cambridge: Alice James Poetry Cooperative, 1981).   44

388   Snow, Don, ed. *Boundaries Carved in Water: An Analysis of River and Water Management in the Upper Missouri Basin* (Missoula: Northern Lights Research and Education Institute, Inc., 1986).   55

389   Snyder, Gary. *Turtle Island* (New York: New Directions, 1974).   78

390   Snyder, Gary. "Good, Wild, Sacred" in *Meeting the Expectations of the Land: Essays in Sustainable Agriculture and Stewardship*, at p. 195, Wes Jackson, Wendell Berry, and Bruce Colman, eds. (San Francisco: North Point Press, 1984).   78

391   *South Dakota Review*, volume 23, No. 4 (1985, edition dedicated to Wallace Stegner).   40

392   Spurr, Stephen H., and Burton V. Barnes. *Forest Ecology* (New York: Wiley, 3d ed. 1980).   64

393   Steen, Harold K. *The United States Forest Service: A History* (Seattle: University of Washington Press, 1976)   47

394   Stegner, Wallace. *Mormon Country* (Lincoln: University of Nebraska Press, 1970; orig. pub., 1942).   44, 57

395   Stegner, Wallace. *The Big Rock Candy Mountain* (New York: Sagamore Press, 1943).   3, 9, 40

BIBLIOGRAPHY

ITEM	AUTHOR & TITLE	PAGE NO.
396	Stegner, Wallace. *Beyond the Hundredth Meridian: John Wesley Powell and the Second Opening of the West* (Boston: Houghton Mifflin, 1954).	9, 20, 35, 39
397	Stegner, Wallace. *Wolf Willow: A History, a Story, and a Memory* (New York: Viking Press, 1962).	14, 40
398	Stegner, Wallace. *The Gathering of Zion: The Story of the Mormon Trail* (New York: McGraw-Hill, 1964).	39, 43, 44
399	Stegner, Wallace. *The Sound of Mountain Water* (Garden City, N.Y.: Doubleday, 1969).	1, 9, 39, 84, 86
400	Stegner, Wallace. *Angle of Repose* (Garden City, N.Y.: Doubleday, 1971).	9, 40, 83
401	Stegner, Wallace. *The Uneasy Chair: A Biography of Bernard DeVoto* (Garden City, N.Y.: Doubleday, 1974).	39
402	Stegner, Wallace. *The Spectator Bird* (Garden City, N.Y.: Doubleday, 1976).	40
403	Stegner, Wallace, ed. *This Is Dinosaur: Echo Park and Its Magic Rivers* (Boulder, Colo.: Roberts Rinehart, 1955).	39
404	Stegner, Wallace, and Richard W. Etulain. *Conversations with Wallace Stegner on Western History and Literature* (Salt Lake City: University of Utah Press, 1983).	40
405	Steinbeck, John. *Tortilla Flat* (New York: Grosset & Dunlap, 1935).	17

ITEM	AUTHOR & TITLE	PAGE NO.
406	Steinbeck, John. *Of Mice and Men* (New York: Modern Library, 1938).	17
407	Steinbeck, John. *The Grapes of Wrath* (New York: Bantam Books, 1955; orig. pub., 1939).	17
408	Steinbeck, John. *Cannery Row* (New York: Viking Press, 1945).	17
409	Steinbeck, John. *East of Eden* (New York: Viking Press, 1952).	17
410	Steiner, Stan. *The Ranchers: A Book of Generations* (New York: Knopf, 1985).	51
411	Stewart, William Morris. *Reminiscences of Senator William M. Stewart of Nevada* (New York: Neale Pub. Co., 1908).	16, 17
412	Stoddart, Laurence A., Arthur D. Smith, and T. Box. *Range Management* (New York: McGraw-Hill, 3d ed. 1975).	63
413	Strickland, Rennard. *Fire and the Spirits: Cherokee Law From Clan to Court* (Norman: University of Oklahoma Press, 1975).	81
414	Stroup, Richard L., and John A. Baden. *Natural Resources: Bureaucratic Myths and Environmental Management* (San Francisco: Pacific Institute for Public Policy Research, 1983).	77, 80
415	Sundborg, George. *Hail Columbia: The Thirty-Year Struggle for Grand Coulee Dam* (New York: Macmillan, 1954).	20

ITEM	AUTHOR & TITLE	PAGE NO.
416	Swadesh, Frances Leon. *Los Primeros Pobladores: Hispanic Americans of the Ute Frontier* (Notre Dame: University of Notre Dame Press, 1974).	43
417	Swisher, Carl B. *Stephen J. Field: Craftsman of the Law* (Hamden, Conn.: Archan Books, 1930).	16
418	Tarling, D. H., ed. *Economic Geology and Geotectonics* (New York: Wiley, 1981).	62
419	Tateishi, John, ed. *And Justice for All: An Oral History of the Japanese American Internment Camps* (New York: Random House, 1984).	45
420	Taylor, Robert Lewis. *The Travels of Jaimie McPheeters* (Garden City, N.Y.: Doubleday, 1958).	16
421	Taylor, Theodore W. *The States and Their Indian Citizens* (Washington, D.C.: U.S. Bureau of Indian Affairs; for sale by the Supt. of Docs., U.S. Govt. Print. Off., 1972).	82
422	Teale, Edwin W. *The Wilderness World of John Muir* (Boston: Houghton Mifflin, 1954).	35, 36, 51
423	Thwaites, Reuben G., ed. *Original Journals of the Lewis & Clark Expedition* (New York: Arno Press, 1969) (eight volumes).	33
424	Treadwell, Edward F. *The Cattle King* (Santa Cruz, Calif.: Western Tanager Press, rev. ed. 1981).	34
425	Trefethen, James B. *An American Crusade for Wildlife* (New York: Winchester Press, 1975).	72

ITEM	AUTHOR & TITLE	PAGE NO.
426	Trennert, Robert A. *Alternative to Extinction: Federal Indian Policy and the Beginnings of the Reservation System, 1846–51* (Philadelphia: Temple University Press, 1975).	23
427	Tuan, Yi-fu. *Space and Place: The Perspective of Experience* (Minneapolis: University of Minnesota Press, 1977).	83
428	Tucker, William. *Progress and Privilege: America in the Age of Environmentalism* (Garden City: N.Y.: Anchor Press/ Doublday, 1982).	79, 85
429	Turner, Frederick Jackson. *The Frontier in American History* (Tucson: University of Arizona Press, 1986; orig. pub., 1920).	13, 29
430	Turner, Frederick W. *Beyond Geography: The Western Spirit Against the Wilderness* (New York: Viking Press, 1980).	30
431	Turner, Frederick W. *Rediscovering America: John Muir in His Time and Ours* (New York: Viking Press, 1985).	36
432	Twain, Mark. *Roughing It* (Berkeley: Published for the Iowa Center for Textual Studies by the University of California Press, 1972; orig. pub., 1872).	16
433	Udall, Stewart L. *The Quiet Crisis* (Salt Lake City: Gibbs-Smith Publisher, 1988; orig. pub., 1963).	39

ITEM	AUTHOR & TITLE	PAGE NO.

434   United States Commission on Wartime Reloca-   **45**
tion and Internment of Civilians. *Personal Justice Denied: Report of the Committee on Wartime
Relocation and Internment of Civilians*
(Washington: The Commission; for sale by
the Supt. of Docs., U.S. Govt. Print. Off., 1983).

435   United States Forest Service, Department of   **64, 65**
Agriculture, *Forest Service, An Analysis of the
Timber Situation in the United States, 1952–2030*
(Washington, D.C.: U.S. Govt. Print. Off.,
1982).

436   *United States v. Grimaud*, 220 U.S. 506 (1911).   **51**

437   United States Water Resource Council. *The   **62**
Nation's Water Resources, Second National
Water Assessment: 1975–2000* (Washington,
D.C.: Water Resources Council; for sale by
the Supt. of Docs., U.S. Govt. Print. Off., 1978).

438   *Utah Power & Light Co. v. United States*, 243 U.S.   **51**
389 (1917).

439   Vallentine, John F. *Range Development and Im-   **63**
provements* (Provo, Utah: Brigham Young
University Press, 2d ed. 1979).

440   Van Kirk, Sylvia. *Many Tender Ties: Women in   **51**
Fur-Trade Society, 1670–1870* (Norman: Univer-
sity of Oklahoma Press, 1980).

441   Victor, Frances F. *The River of the West: The Ad-   **50**
ventures of Joe Meek* (Missoula: Mountain
Press Pub. Co., 1983; orig. pub., 1870).

ITEM	AUTHOR & TITLE	PAGE NO.
442	Wallace, David R. *The Klamath Knot: Explorations of Myth and Evolution* (San Francisco: Sierra Club Books, 1983).	69, 85
443	Washburn, Wilcomb E. *The Indian in America* (New York: Harper & Row, 1975).	30, 81
444	Waters, Frank. *The Man Who Killed the Deer* (Chicago: Sage Books, 1970; orig. pub., 1942).	41, 42
445	Waters, Frank. *The Colorado* (New York: Rinehart, 1946).	54
446	Waters, Frank. *Book of the Hopi* (New York: Viking Press, 1963).	42
447	Waters, Frank. *The Woman at Otowi Crossing* (Denver: A. Swallow, 1966).	54
448	Watkins, T. H. *The Grand Colorado: The Story of a River and Its Canyons* (Palo Alto, Calif.: American West Pub. Co., 1969).	54
449	Watkins, T. H. *On the Shore of the Sundown Sea* (San Francisco: Sierra Club Books, 1973).	58, 72
450	Watkins, T. H., and Charles S. Watson. *The Lands No One Knows: America and the Public Domain* (San Francisco: Sierra Club Books, 1975).	9, 18
451	Weatherford, Gary D., and F. Lee Brown, eds. *New Courses for the Colorado River: Major Issues for the Next Century* (Albuquerque: University of New Mexico Press, 1986).	54

ITEM	AUTHOR & TITLE	PAGE NO.
452	Weatherford, Gary D., F. Lee Brown, Helen Ingram, and Dean Mann, eds. *Water and Agriculture in the Western United States: Conservation, Reallocation and Markets* (Boulder, Colo.: Westview Press, 1982).	63
453	Webb, Walter Prescott. *The Great Plains* (Boston: Ginn, 1931).	5, 9, 18, 30, 55
454	Weber, David J. *The Mexican Frontier, 1821–1846: The American Southwest Under Mexico* (Albuquerque: University of New Mexico Press, 1982).	23
455	Weber, David J., ed. *Foreigners in Their Native Land: Historical Roots of the Mexican Americans* (Albuquerque: University of New Mexico Press, 1973).	24, 42
456	Weglyn, Michi. *Years of Infamy: The Untold Story of America's Concentration Camps* (New York: W. Morrow, 1976).	45
457	Welch, James. *Winter in the Blood* (New York: Harper & Row, 1974).	41
458	Western Literature Association. *A Literary History of the American West* (Fort Worth: Texas Christian University Press, 1987).	xii, 73
459	Westphall, Victor. *Thomas Benton Catron and His Era* (Tucson: University of Arizona Press, 1973).	24, 35
460	Wilderness Society. *Conserving Biological Diversity in our National Forests* (Washington, D.C.: The Wilderness Society, 1986).	69

ITEM	AUTHOR & TITLE	PAGE NO.
461	Wiley, Peter, and Robert Gottlieb. *Empires in the Sun: The Rise of the New American West* (New York: Putnam, 1982).	21, 29, 49
462	Wilkinson, Charles F. *American Indians, Time, and the Law: Native Societies in a Modern Constitutional Democracy* (New Haven: Yale University Press, 1987).	81
463	Wilkinson, Charles F., and H. Michael Anderson, *Land and Resource Planning in the National Forests* (Washington, D.C.: Island Press, 1987).	47
464	Wilkinson, Charles F. "The Law of the American West: A Critical Bibliography of the Nonlegal Sources," *Michigan Law Review*, volume 85, at p. 953 (1987).	xiii
465	Wilkinson, Charles F. *The Eagle Bird: Searching for an Ethic of Place* (Salt Lake City: Howe Bros., 1989).	83
466	Williams, Terry Tempest. *Pieces of White Shell: A Journey to Navajoland* (New York: Scribner's, 1984).	83
467	Wilson, James. *Groundwater: A Non-Technical Guide* (Philadelphia: Academy of Natural Sciences, 1982).	70
468	Wister, Owen. *The Virginian: A Horseman of the Plains* (New York: Macmillan, 1904).	26
469	Withers, Bruce, and Stanley Vipond. *Irrigation: Design and Practice* (Ithaca, N.Y.: Cornell University Press, 2d ed. 1980).	63

BIBLIOGRAPHY

ITEM	AUTHOR & TITLE	PAGE NO.
470	Wolfe, Linnie M. *Son of the Wilderness: The Life of John Muir* (New York: Knopf, 1945).	36
471	Worster, Donald. *Rivers of Empire: Water, Aridity, and the Growth of the American West* (New York: Pantheon Books, 1986).	21, 27, 30
472	Wright, William H. *The Grizzly Bear: The Narrative of a Hunter-Naturalist* (New York: Scribner, 1909).	66
473	Wunder, John R., ed. *Working the Range: Essays on the History of Western Land Management and the Environment* (Westport, Conn.: Greenwood Press, 1985).	63
474	Wyant, William K. *Westward in Eden: The Public Lands and the Conservation Movement* (Berkeley: University of California Press, 1982).	29
475	Young, Mary E. *Redskins, Ruffleshirts, and Rednecks: Indian Allotments in Alabama and Mississippi: 1830–1860* (Norman: University of Oklahoma Press, 1961).	20
476	Young, Stanley Paul, and Edward A. Goldman. *The Wolves of North America* (Washington, D.C.: American Wildlife Institute, 1944) (two volumes).	67
477	Zaslowsky, Dyan, and the Wilderness Society. *These American Lands: Parks, Wilderness, and the Public Lands* (New York: Holt, 1986).	29

ITEM	AUTHOR & TITLE	PAGE NO.
478	Zolbrod, Paul G. *Diné Bahanè: The Navajo Creation Story* (Albuquerque: University of New Mexico Press, 1984).	48
479	Zwinger, Ann. *Wind in the Rock* (New York: Harper & Row, 1978).	54

General References

ITEM	AUTHOR & TITLE	PAGE NO.

480   Etulain, Richard W. *A Bibliographical Guide to the Study of Western American Literature* (Lincoln: University of Nebraska Press, 1982).   xii, 73

481   Lamar, Howard R. *The Reader's Encyclopedia of the American West* (New York: Thomas Y. Crowell, 1977).   xii

482   Malone, Michael P. *Historians and the American West* (Lincoln: University of Nebraska Press, 1983).   xii, 15

483   Nichols, Roger L. *American Frontier and Western Issues: A Historiographical Review* (Westport, Conn.: Greenwood Press, 1986).   xii, 15

484   Paul, Rodman W. and Richard W. Etulain. *The Frontier and the American West* (Arlington Heights, Ill.: AHM Publishing, 1977).   xii

485   Smith, Dwight L. *The American and Canadian West: A Bibliography* (Santa Barbara: Clio Press, 1979).   xii

486   Tuska, Jon and Vicki Piekarski. *The Frontier Experience: A Reader's Guide to the Life and Literature of the American West* (Jefferson, N.C.: McFarland, 1984).   xii, 15

487   Valk, Barbara G. *Borderline: A Bibliography of the United States–Mexico Borderlands* (Los Angeles: UCLA Latin American Center, 1988).   xii, 24, 42

ITEM	AUTHOR & TITLE	PAGE NO.
488	Wagner, Henry R. and Charles L. Camp. *The Plains and the Rockies: A Critical Bibliography of Exploration, Adventure and Travel in the American West, 1800–1865* (San Francisco: John Howell-Books, 1982).	xii